"Children express the innocence and
loveliness of heaven's beauty."

Letters from Heaven

Volume VI
Laudem Gloriae

authorHOUSE®

AuthorHouse™
1663 Liberty Drive
Bloomington, IN 47403
www.authorhouse.com
Phone: 1 (800) 839-8640

Published by AuthorHouse 03/20/2019

ISBN: 978-1-5462-6182-7 (sc)
ISBN: 978-1-5462-6181-0 (e)

Print information available on the last page.

Any people depicted in stock imagery provided by Getty Images are models, and such images are being used for illustrative purposes only. Certain stock imagery © Getty Images.

This book is printed on acid-free paper.

Because of the dynamic nature of the Internet, any web addresses or links contained in this book may have changed since publication and may no longer be valid. The views expressed in this work are solely those of the author and do not necessarily reflect the views of the publisher, and the publisher hereby disclaims any responsibility for them.

"Those who honor Me
I will honor."

This book is dedicated to
St. John Gabriel Perboyre
(1802-1840)
a Vincentian missionary priest
that was brutally tortured and martyred
for his faith in China
on September 11, 1840.

He quietly suffered a most cruel martyrdom.
He was beaten and scourged twenty times,
Yet he refused to stomp on a crucifix.
His face was branded with the words,
"Teacher of False Religions"
And he was condemned
To be strangled on a cross.

Although little is remembered of his life,
Jesus wants his name
to be known and honored
for his great life sacrifice.

"Divine Savior, transform me into Yourself.
May my feet be Your feet.
May my hands be Your hands.
May my eyes be Your eyes.
May my ears be Your ears.
May my mouth be Your mouth.
May my mind think Your thoughts.
May my perspective be Your perspective.
Grant that every faculty of my body
may serve only to glorify You.
Above all, transform my soul and all
its powers that my memory, my will,
and my affections may be the memory,
the will, and the affections of You.
I beg You to destroy everything in me
that is not of You.
I pray that I may live in complete union
with you so that I may say with St. Paul,
"I live, but not I; Christ lives in me."

St. John Gabriel Perboyre
(January 6, 1802 - September 11, 1840)

April 21, 2015

"Moments of great beauty come in life to lift the heart to the eternal homeland. Heaven is a forever land of beauty, goodness, joy, and bliss. All those counted worthy to live there eternally are the blessed children of a holy God.

From eternity you have been chosen to inherit this destiny. There was never a time that I did not know your name or see your face. You have been in My heart forever. Could there be anything more glorious?

You are My eternal thought, coming forth from My Being. That is why I tell you that we are one, for you have been with Me before you were ever created. How could you exist if I had not created you?

Man cannot understand My infinite capacity. I cannot be encompassed for I AM. I made Myself one of you to break the barrier of our division. I limited Myself to an earthly body to communicate Myself to you more fully.

If only souls would understand My loving condescension, beyond your mind's grasp! I ask you to be obedient only to open your soul to holiness, for without holiness no man can see God.

I am not a God of rules and regulations. I am a God of holy love, seeking to transform My broken children into saints forever beholding My omnipotent glory.

All you that will try to understand My heart will be blessed with eyes to see. The rewards of a holy and loving life are endless and beautiful.

O children, discipline yourselves to seek eternal treasures. You will be blessed beyond your dreams or imaginings.

Use this short life to seek My face. I will reveal Myself to you and you will die in the arms of your great Friend. Your death will be beautiful, without fear, for I will hold you in My arms and you will wake up in a world of stunning beauty.

Then you will truly say: "It was worth it to follow Jesus."

Jesus,
Lover of Your Soul

April 23, 2015

"Only one thing is needful in your life and that is your open heart to obey, love, and serve Me. If I have created you, it should be your duty to requite My generosity by your obedience to the designs I have for your existence.

Souls run through life thinking that all happens by chance. The sun, the rain, the crops that bring forth food from dirt – humanity believes these are accidental causes, always existing, with no thought for how they came to be. Man takes absolutely everything for granted!

If I did not keep the globe in a revolving pattern, your world would collapse in one moment. If the atmosphere of your earth was altered in any way, all mankind would die immediately. If the rain stayed in the clouds, you would starve. Does man ever stop to wonder how these things keep working in such an excellent way?

How futile the thoughts of men! There is no eye for the big picture. He stays embedded in the petty things of life living in the cage of his restricted mindset. How foolish! Even a child has the sense to know that a Creator lovingly fashioned the earth.

A child sees the blade of grass, the bubble in the pond, the insect on a leaf. The adults in this generation see cars and phones and televisions and bank statements. They have lost their vision for the important things in the world.

Prestige, popularity, beauty, fame – enrapturing allurements to deaden the soul to heaven's beauty on earth.

Science, religions cropping up daily, hedonism, intellectualism, psychology, entertainment – false images of the reality of God in the world.

Listen to the children call you back to the beauty of the earth. Get out of your cramped houses, your bleak buildings, your reclusive entertainments. Run out into nature. Raise your eyes to the heavens and ask God to restore your vision for what really matters – the eternal reality of God.

The angels play among the landscapes of your earth. Nature is My kingdom on earth to them. Open your doors to the light of nature, My children. Get out of your closed houses where you sit gazing at an electronic propaganda box.

Go outside to see if you can see My angels outside your door. Only eyes that have acquired the vision of a child can see them.

Trust Me; they are there."

Jesus,
Angel Lover

March 4, 2015

"That shall stand what God hath wrought." All things consist because of My life breath. Man thinks he is the owner of the world. Man owns nothing, not even his next breath. His life is a vapor, a mist; here today, gone and forgotten tomorrow. His toil will not be remembered. His life work will be discarded. His belongings will be bought and sold. His family members will move forward. Life is continual growth and change. No man can stop the cycle.

A wise man will question his priorities. He will look to the end of his life for answers on how to live his life today. He will wisely consider that he was created to glorify his Creator, not to fulfill his own desires. He will sacrifice what is set before him for the greater good.

"Man is born to trouble, as sparks fly upward." Every man bears a burden in this world, whether rich or poor. It is the lot of man to suffer in this world. Though he may run from it, it pursues him relentlessly, finally catching up with him. It is better to take up your cross obediently rather than to let it catch you unawares, trampling you beneath its weight.

God's ways are strange to the heart of man. Who would dream that suffering would lead to glory? Only a God beyond our realm of comprehension. Our job as a human is to obey this God beyond our realm of thought, by faith to blindly trust in Him, following Him obediently through life's twists and turns. He knows the path He has marked out for you.

Your death day will come, man of earth. Will you be prepared to meet your God? He is the God that gave you every day as a gift. He wanted you to live a full life, rejoicing in His presence. Will you welcome death, or will it be a day of terror for you?

Reconsider your life and make the necessary changes. Today is your gift to do just that."

Jesus,
Life Giver

June 19, 2017

"The duty of the scribe is to record the words of his teacher, to memorialize these words for generations to come. Even in these days, I have My scribes, souls of faith that record My words to them.

My revelation is eternal, for I change not. I am the same yesterday, today, and forever. I cannot be put into a box of man's limited thinking. I speak when I will to whomever I will for My own highest purposes.

Those of little faith are incredulous and cynical, but My simple souls of understanding know and hear My voice.

My voice speaks through all of creation in a language beyond man's ability to hear. Man is trapped in his body which is a barrier to true life, the life of spirit. This shell cordons him off from the vastness of the universe and its workings. Only spiritual communion opens up this corridor into God's world of infinity.

There are no words to describe who God is. Infinite and omnipresent are shell terms. Man has no words to describe God. He cannot be described in words. He is a force that illuminates all that is. He is light. He is love.

God waits for those who seek to find Him. As the Eternal Father, He lovingly watches over all that He has created. He is pervasive love dropping as honey over everything living. He embellishes all things with His glittering light. He is mist and clouds and diamonds and volcanic smoke.

He is laughter and joy and mirth. He is the peace overlooking the pond in the dense forest, the place no man has ever seen.

He is eternal stillness, delightful beauty, and glorious beatitude.

To see Him you must reach out both arms to love Him. Open yourself to His beautiful and fatherly embrace. Bask in the bounteous beauty of this earth He created so lovingly and meticulously.

Speak your words of love to Him. Settle into His heart. He loves you with an infinite and eternal love.

God is in your hands to love and adore. He has given Himself to you. Receive His offered love to you."

Jesus,
God's Love in Human Form

March 5, 2015

"To live with Me, to walk daily with Me by your side, is to live a beautiful day. You will have new eyes to see the world around you. You will be aware of My creative artistry in everything.

I walked with Adam and Eve in the cool of the day enjoying their friendship and their response to My love. Our days were beautiful together until they were broken by disobedience and rebellion. They lost faith in My goodness and sought to separate themselves from My counsels. This wounded My heart. Like the father of the prodigal son, I had to let them go.

Even today, so many souls run from My friendship. I want to walk beside all of you today to give you a beautiful day. All it takes is a glance in My direction and I will run to you, as the father of the prodigal son ran in joyful anticipation to meet his son.

I am your Father. I created you. I know everything about you, all your desires and heartfelt needs. I want to help you become the best person you can be on this earth, but you have to allow it. I am held at arm's length even by many of My faithful children.

Come closer to Me, children of My heart. I am always calling you. "Draw near to God and He will draw near to you." Joyfully I will clasp your hand and we shall walk together on your journey of life. Our friendship will grow with each passing day.

When it is time for you to leave this earth to come to My world, you will peacefully close your eyes and I will carry you over the threshold. You will awaken to a new land of glorious beauty.

Trust Me, children. Give Me your hand. Let's walk your remaining days on earth together."

Jesus,
Friend

March 19, 2015

"To come to the fountain of all wisdom with an eager spirit is the greatest grace from your God. God is drawing you to Himself with His gentle cords of love. So few respond to His embraces and caresses.

To love God with all your heart is His delight. He desires to have loving children surrounding His glorious throne. His peaceful creation is a glorious foretaste of the glory of heaven. All reign there in peace and contentment, basking in the love of God.

Man races through time, seeking adventures. The greatest adventure in a lifetime is to plumb the depths of God.

To sit alone with God, silently pondering His creativity and merciful artistic splendors is to magnify His attributes, to render homage to the Creator of all that exists. To walk alone with God in loving communion is the greatest of all joys on earth.

God desires to walk in the garden of each soul He has so lovingly created. His designs are all of love, to craft a magnificent masterpiece studded in holy splendor. Man was made to walk with God. In this lies all his happiness. Man needs a loving Father to guide his path on earth. He needs a Consoler, a Friend, a Creator to answer his questions.

Why does man forsake his own mercy? Why does he hide from God like Adam in the first garden?

Man was made for fellowship with his Creator. Without this connection, he is lost. His happiness lies in his heart of obedient love and commitment.

If only man understood the beautiful plans in God's heart!"

Jesus,
Son of the God of Love

January 11, 2018

"Holiness of life is so rare on the earth. It takes time, silence, and solitude to grow in holiness. There is no silence or solitude on earth except on the sickbed or at death's door. How sad at the moment of death to realize you were never alone with God getting to know Him!

To remain silently in God's presence is the path to a holy life on earth. Without time in God's holy presence, it is impossible to live a holy life.

The world devours its inhabitants with everything that appeals to the senses. There is a fear of solitude and silence. It appears empty and meaningless to mankind. That is why My ways are not your ways. I see everything differently. My world is another realm, something your humanity cannot understand unless there is spiritual revelation and illumination.

It is not your acquired knowledge on earth that helps you grow in holiness. It is the silent times of revelation when God diffuses Himself into your heart. That is when you truly come to know God – in the stillness alone before Him.

Who takes the time to spend time alone with God in this fast-paced life? Very few. But those that do are greatly blessed. That is the secret of life that so few have found – the pearl of great price – capturing God's heart in the silence.

The angels wait in a holy hush when a purified soul sits patiently before God Most High. They fold their wings in adoring prayer before this meeting of flesh and Spirit.

God has so highly favored men to impart His divinity to them, the Holy Spirit's embrace. He has not done this with the angels. God became a human, which mystified the angelic hosts. In wonderment, they beheld God become man on earth. What dignity was conferred on humankind!

How Satan destroys the dignity of man incessantly. Satan hates and despises human beings because they are a receptacle of God's image. If only they knew the possibilities of allowing God to manifest Himself on earth through their lowly bodies of earth dust.

Let God fill your earthly body with His glory. Radiate God's presence on earth by allowing Him to live His holy life in you. It is His work to make you holy. It is impossible for you, but with God, all things are possible."

The Wonder of Heaven

April 2, 2018

"Dreams come and go like a mist in the morning fog, but My path is a true path leading to life eternally in God's presence. Man is a dream maker on earth. He constantly talks of fulfilling and chasing his dreams, but many of these dreams are his own self-fulfilling desires that will vanish before the light of the sun in the end.

The only true dreams to follow are the dreams that God has planned for your existence. He alone knows what plans and purposes will truly give you the joy and fulfillment you so earnestly seek.

Man has made his self-professed dreams his idols in this age. The dream to be rich, to be famous, to be praised, to be the best at something ... This is not God's way of the cross.

Jesus stated: "Not My will but Thine be done." He truly gave up His dreams for the will of His Father. He had no other ambition than to be conformed to His Father's perfect will and plan for His life. "I came not to do My own will, but the will of the One Who sent Me."

All this talk of dreams is a delusion, especially to the youth. Their heads are filled with dreams of fame and glory, most of them completely unattainable in this life. They run and chase these phantom dreams for years until they reach adulthood and then they grow cynical and bitter.

They feel life has fooled them. They turn to things that will dull their sense of failure to forget the wasted years and foolish dreams.

My dream for you is sanctification and holiness of life, purity to stand before God's presence undefiled and unspotted by the useless dreams of the world that delude souls. Your dream should be an eternal dream – the saving of your soul unto life eternal where your true dreams will be fully realized.

Do not let the world's systems delude you, men of earth. The world has nothing to offer you but fleeting pleasure, which is not lasting or sustainable while on earth.

Look to Me to dream dreams that are real and eternal. God is your final dream. When you face Him, you will never need to dream again."

Jesus,
The Holy Spirit's Mouth

January 19, 2018

"I have given My friends on earth the great gift of being able to enter God's presence with their requests. I have opened the door to the throne room by My redemptive death. This door was closed to man for centuries. Sin blocked the entrance. My death and resurrection broke the barrier door down. I brought My brothers and sisters with Me through that door into God's holy presence. My Blood covered their iniquities. What a triumph!

The door is open, but souls have become complacent and disinterested. They are too busy living their lives on earth to talk to God. They do not understand the price paid for this holy entrance into God's presence. They will not even walk through the door of prayer to talk to their Father-Creator whose love reconciled them to Himself.

My gift is spurned by the majority of mankind. This is grievous. "Men loved darkness rather than light because their deeds were evil." To walk through the door of prayer into God's presence is no small thing.

God's omnipotence is at your service. God's love will surround you with a holy joy. All that is good is found in this place – peace, love, joy, contentment, purpose, and miracles.

Prayer is the answer to the world's evil. Only God can quell the terrible tide of evil that has swept over the world. Recourse to God is the answer to every problem in the world but "men loved darkness rather than light."

Those who pray on earth are few. The Evil One continually harasses them because he knows their power with God to change things on earth. It is a holy perseverance they must endure.

By prayer, you can change the world. "The effectual fervent prayer of a righteous man availeth much." Those that persevere in prayer in crossing the threshold into God's presence, become ambassadors on earth. They represent man's needs to God. They pass from heaven to earth to effect change. Theirs is a holy ambassadorship. They truly make lasting change on the earth.

It is very hard to stay true to the course of prayer. Many fall by the wayside, but those that persevere are true warriors for God, chosen souls bearing God's children on their heart into God's presence. They shall be rewarded."

Jesus,
Prayer Warrior Par Excellence

February 4, 2015

"To be able to communicate all that I am to a soul is a resting place for My need to love. Man is so involved with himself that He doesn't realize My need to express My love. As I <u>am</u> Love, My life is love. How do you think I must feel when My life of love is unrequited?

If only man could turn away from himself to look at Me. What glorious wonders he would find! As I am all that exists, can you even begin to imagine what it must be like to live in Me constantly? Then you could truly say that all things are yours in Christ.

My true friends are those that spend time with Me. They turn away from themselves to look at Me for at least a few moments of their day. They do not forget Me for useless trifles. In Me are hidden all the riches of your existence. How could you live apart from Me, who am life?

Again I say to you, man forsakes his greatest good by abandoning his Creator. Only the wise in heart have understood the importance of communing with Me daily heart to heart. They acquire inestimable riches in My presence.

The world sees this time spent with Me as a leisurely waste of time, yet in reality, these souls are gathering precious graces and are distributing them throughout the earth by their prayers. Is this a waste of time, to save souls by your hidden quality time with Me, gathering My graces in your arms to distribute to your brothers?

Once again, children, I urge you not to forsake your own mercy by abandoning your Creator for the thrills set before you on earth. They are deceptive devices to steal your eternal inheritance from your hands.

Seek the eternal. Seek the gates of heaven. Seek your God who incessantly cries out for your love."

Jesus,
Spirit's Call

January 21, 2015

"Another day is before you. How will you live it? When you lay your head on your pillow tonight, what thoughts will you have about how you spent your day? Time is My gift to you. It is precious and is used to inherit eternal treasure. How souls waste this precious gift!

Souls feel that time spent sitting quietly thinking is wasted time. They prefer activity, plans, and goals. They have to keep moving constantly, never allowing their minds to rest in My company. If they would allow Me to speak to them unhindered, they would learn many beautiful things that would make life more meaningful and precious.

Life is to be revered. A lifetime is a holy gift given by an infinite God. How many souls use this gift of life the way the Creator God intended it to be used? Sadly, very few. Man pursues futile interests. He forsakes his own mercy. How grievous!

As you sit quietly with Me, My light descends upon you, beautifying your spirit and your countenance. Heavenly beams spread a glorious aura around your person.

In My days on earth, souls knew that My apostles had spent time with Me. It is the same today. Souls know in the depths of their beings when they see a soul beautified by the presence of time spent with Jesus.

There is a subtle light surrounding one of My own, those that bask in My presence. Peacefulness of countenance, a noble bearing, and compassionate eyes mark My chosen ones.

Thank you, my children, for coming here to be with Me in My sacramental presence. I am alone much of the time as souls explore the world.

You who come to commune with Me here are greatly blessed."

Jesus,
Lonely Love

June 22, 2017

"You can tune into the spiritual vibrations of the universe at any time you desire. Your part is to quiet yourself, to find solitude, to rest trustfully in My presence. That is when I can speak to you freely. When you listen to the silence, it speaks to you in its own language, the language that is disappearing from the earth. Wherever man invades, he drives out the silent language.

Man brings noise with him wherever he goes. It is his backpack which he carries so faithfully. He never sets it down, but unknowingly carries this heavy burden all the days of his life. Only in death will he recognize this weight strapped to his back. He must put it down then. It was the unrecognized traveler, burdening him unnecessarily, vigilantly keeping him from looking at his life or communicating with the world of spirit.

A quiet man is beautiful to behold in God's eyes. "Precious in the eyes of God is a meek and quiet spirit."

Animals speak the language of silence. They are not burdened with word baggage. They exist for the praise and glory of God, glorifying Him by their quiet existence.

Gentleness and silence belong together. One proceeds from the other. There are no inflammatory words to pierce the air ... only peaceful silence and acceptance.

A silent person has captured his will in his hands and holds it captive. His will no longer controls him. He sails through life calmly on peaceful seas of growth. He exerts no pressure on any situation. He has become master of all things by controlling his tongue.

Souls, can you find this world of silent existence, praising God by your acquiescence to all that He brings into your life? Can you join the animal world by existing for God's glory alone, not exerting yourself, but losing yourself in the process?

The wisest souls are the most silent. They have recognized their place in the universe. To be God's child, you must learn His language of silence.

Monasteries are overflowing with God's children, subservient to His silent call. God dwells there in peace among the silent ones."

The Holy Spirit,
Caller of Silent Souls

January 1, 2017

"The soul that has learned to rest in God is the soul that has matured in God's love. On the seventh day God rested in all His works. Even so, a child of God can rest in the works of God. To rest in the love of God is the highest calling, a call beyond all your works. Your deeds are an overflow of your rest in the presence of God.

Man does things backwards. Man thinks he pleases Me first by deeds. No. It is the heart I desire above the deeds. If I possess the heart, the deeds will flow from our union.

How do I possess the heart? We become a love-union. We are fused together in love. The bond of our love produces a holy life that pours forth good deeds.

In your silent learning moments you acquire My gentleness. You learn to deal with souls as I do. I instruct with meekness, kindness, and gentleness. I do not judge or coerce. I pull souls to My heart with My cords of lovingkindness. You must do the same. Souls cannot resist My love. They are drawn to the power of love. It ignites a fire in the heart that seeks to be kindled incessantly.

God's love is a forever consuming flame. The fire never dies throughout eternity. Only those inflamed with the fire of God's love can change the world. All else is naught. Many works are being done in My name that are barren and dry without My love covering. These will burn up in the day of judgment.

How can you change the world? Fall in love with your God who loves you beyond your imaginative powers. Throw wood on the fire of your love by proclaiming your love to Me in your heart. Keep Me at the center of all you do. Remember Me in all things.

This is how you throw wood on the fire of our love affair.

Remember Me as I remember you."

Jesus,
God's Memory

January 4, 2018

"Another day … another opportunity to draw closer to your God, to get to know Him, to learn what pleases Him, to understand His heart of tenderness toward all that exists.

God is beyond your realm of thought, yet He can reveal Himself to you to your capacity to understand. "Draw near to God and He will draw near to you." To draw near means to cleanse yourself of impurities that you may draw near to the holiness of God. His pure gaze burns up all that is impure.

God is the Eternal Child – all-pure, all-innocent, all-loving. There is no deceit or duplicity in Him. His gaze of candor surveys the earth in tenderness, hovering as a mother hen over her newborn chicks.

He has been greatly misunderstood and maligned by humankind. They call Him severe and judgmental, yet He is a tender parent gently caressing those He has created. He must use punishment to keep souls from destroying themselves eternally. His judgments are His mercy. Throughout the endless and eternal ages, men will bless God for the trials and afflictions that kept them turning to God in their despair.

This is an eternal play. It doesn't stop at death. It continues forever. Man's soul was created for eternity. He is in the first act of the play which determines his eternal garment of glory.

Blessed are those who have eyes for God on this earth! They are God's chosen ones, His children of predilection, the apple of His eye. They are safeguarded and hidden in His heart of love. They are His brilliant jewels of glory displaying His stupendous grace and mercy.

Who could imagine a God sacrificing Himself for His creations that have rejected Him? Only a God of pure love could do such a glorious thing to redeem man from eternal damnation, which he deserved in his rebellion against righteousness.

God is love. With your love, you draw Him to yourself. He loves to gather His children in His embrace. He loves to see His children smiling and content.

So few souls think of Him! Be one of the few!"

Jesus,
God's Ambassador

January 6, 2017

"A willing heart knows no boundaries. An open heart, ready to love Me beyond the world's treasures, becomes a channel of grace to the world. I cannot penetrate a closed heart. I do not come where I am not welcome. When you open your heart to Me, I descend in all My glory, transforming your being into a spectacle of heaven's glory on earth.

I am looking for the heart of a child to reveal Myself to the nations. My greatest icons of grace, My saints, were holy children following My parental guidance. They owned nothing of themselves but acknowledged all as gift and grace. Their eyes anxiously reached to heaven for all direction and guidance. They never sought fame, riches, or glory. They looked for My approval in all their actions.

These holy children changed their environment. They tore down carefully constructed plans to build towers of human endeavors. They humbled themselves as loving children in every situation. I will use a child to bring down Satan's edifices of deception. Little David will defeat Goliath by his innocence and purity.

Do not be anxious or afraid. Live your life loving Me one moment at a time. I will heal you; I will help you; I will lead you; I will guide you. It will not be you ... it will be I, the Eternal Child, leading the nations to righteousness.

The story is not over, My people. I am doing a new thing on the earth in these days. Evil has raged through the land covering the earth in darkness. I am rising up to scatter the darkness for I am the Light of life.

"By Me all things consist." I am the King of nations and will take My rightful place of authority over the wickedness in high places.

It is to you to humble yourselves and pray, My children. Strongholds are brought down by prayer and fasting. Leave the rest to Me."

Jesus,
Tired of Satan's Evil

January 6, 2018

"My hands of mercy are outstretched to you. "He that cometh to Me I will in no wise cast out." I am the great and powerful Creator, yet I reach out My hands and My heart to the weak little children in your world.

Relax in Me and let Me take care of you. Things go smoothly when you do not get in the way of My workings within your life. "All things work for <u>good</u> to those that love God." Even My love is My gift to you.

Praise and rejoice when you feel fearful and weak. Show forth your trust in Me when you are afraid. Let Me fill you with My peace and serenity.

You are a chosen vessel to show forth My praise. Your song was My gift to you. I knew this gift would not be wasted in the world's system. It is dedicated to Me, and how pleased this makes Me.

My child, trust in My help. Do not fear; TRUST. All will be well. "This is the day the Lord has made. Rejoice and be glad in it." Rejoicing and fearfulness do not mix. Praise and timidity do not gel. Trust and distrust do not walk hand in hand. Give me your heart and I will transform it into confidence. "Do not fear. It is My pleasure to give you the kingdom."

God,
Your Father in Heaven

January 3, 2018

"If you take the time to listen, you will hear My voice within your heart. I bring you words of love, peace, and My joy. I truly am all thing to all men. I fulfill your deepest longings.

My glory hides within your body of flesh. You are the temple of the Holy Spirit. Holiness untapped resides within you. My omnipotent power lies latent within you. You must tap into this Source within you which truly is "Christ in you, the hope of glory."

Sin and obstinacy block My entrance. I cannot freely move about in a heart cluttered with worldly desires and obsessions. I am stifled within a heart given over to the sensual. My Spirit is grieved by a hardened heart that has turned away from My advances. I seek a pure and simple gaze of love. I desire friendship and intimacy, walking earth's paths together in holy harmony ... friends forever on the journey to eternity.

It is so simple. Take My hand held out to you. Come with Me into the realm of spirit, the true reality. You must leave your senses behind and retire calmly within your heart where I am waiting for you eagerly. We will have intimate communion and fellowship when you allow Me to reveal Myself to you. You have a glorious eternity awaiting you. Begin now to enjoy it."

Jesus, Time Traveler

January 10, 2018

"Little ones, all things come to an end. This, too, shall pass. All is coming quickly to its fulfillment in your lives. These are the days of struggle to keep your heads above water. Keep treading the waves. I am with you. Call out to Me when you feel you are sinking beneath the burdens of life. I am always here ready to help you.

All is well. All is not lost. This is all part of the great plan I had in mind for you before your birth on planet earth. Trust in My ways and My judgment.

My heart is always with your heart. I have called you here to commune with you. Most blessed are those that God has called to Himself.

There is a big wide world out there filled with people that have not been blessed as you have. Do not murmur and complain. It is unbecoming to such a favored child of God. Bless, thank, and praise God that you are doing as well as you are surrounded by so many temptations and distractions.

Many souls have fallen by the wayside and have quit bearing spiritual fruits that glorify God. You are moving forward slowly, to be sure, but you haven't left the highway of holiness to seek the roads of the world as many have.

I am proud of you, My children. Though you don't believe it, I know your efforts and your sincere desire to please Me. How can I not respond to a soul that seeks My face?

I desire to comfort and encourage you on your lonely walk to heaven. You feel alone, but you are "surrounded with so great a cloud of witnesses" that have walked the path before you and have been found faithful. Ask for their intercession. They are always before the throne of God interceding for the holy ones.

Keep pressing on. All is well. Keep smiling. All is well. Keep pursuing holiness without which no one will see God.

I am yours and you are Mine. Always remember My great promises to you. I keep My word."

Jesus,
Ambassador for God's Holy Kingdom

January 15, 2018

"All I ask for is your efforts. You will fail and fall repeatedly, but it is in the repentant act of being sorrowful and confessing your sins that I can then forgive you and grant you the grace to go forward.

My love understands your weaknesses. Souls all carry different burdens. I ask My children to allow Me to carry the yoke of the burden beside you. Lean on Me more in time of trouble. Turn to Me in great faith and expect the help of a loving parent.

I am not displeased with you as you are with yourself. I see grace forming you into My likeness little by little, day by day, like the growth of a slow-growing tree, imperceptible but sure.

The spiritual life is a very rocky road of ups and downs. The goal is to stay the course, knowing I am beside you beckoning you to the sanctified life of God.

Little ones, all is well. Calm down. God knows your burdens. He does not allow you to be tempted above your strength level. God fashions saints through trials and tribulations. Each trial is a ladder reaching to heaven that you may reach maturity and sanctity.

Those that come to Me for instruction are the wise ones living in the world. I will never ignore your requests for grace and holiness, but you must know that a saint's path is arduous. Only the strong survive the onslaught of life's woes. You will be strong if you abide in Me.

Love Me. The more you love Me, the holier you will be. Keep your focus on looking into My eyes incessantly.
I am your help and your strength."

Jesus,
God's Love

January 16, 2015

"Do you think these hours spent alone with Me are fruitless? So many things call you to their attention, but these things of earth are transient and fleeting. They have no eternal value. Your treasure in life is your time spent with Me, sitting in My presence, desiring to discern My will for your existence on earth.

I have called My children to Myself to bare My heart to them. In a world covered with filthy imaginations, I seek a pure heart to divulge My intentions.

In every age, there have been so few souls that have taken My mandates seriously. Life called to them as sirens in the night. They turned back in the day of battle. The uphill climb to heaven was too rigorous for them. They fell back to a life of ease and comfort, in harmony with the world's ways.

I am calling out a people for Myself in these last days. They are humble and unknown to the world, hidden away in prayer closets. Heaven knows them well and the saints pray fervently for them. They are holding high the banners of the Christ in the world war against evil.

The last days are upon you, men of earth. The battle is fervent and heated. You must go to the enemy camps to deliver your imprisoned brothers. You have My power to break the chains of bondage that torture and condemn them.

As you go forth in the power of My Spirit, My light will shine before you, making your way plain. It will be <u>My</u> strength that will precede you. My light and power within you will set souls free.

I am gathering My elect for the last battle. Only those souls that have been transformed in My presence will have the strength and fortitude to rescue souls from the power of Satan in these final days."

Jesus, Warrior-King

January 18, 2016

"Moments of reflection in the power and presence of My uplifting and empowering Holy Spirit...

The Spirit of Christ invades pure and empty souls waiting to be filled with the divinity of Jesus. A soul filled with the odor of the world cannot be filled with the fragrance of the perfume of the Christ. Holiness seeks a humble and lowly valley in the spirit. Only the childlike find My holy words of wisdom and retain them in their spirits.

My love exposes souls to the sufferings in the world. Love cannot remain aloof and silent. Love must intervene. Love must come to the rescue. Love must help.

Prayer is your love cry for humanity. Prayer is your lifeline to My heart of love for souls. I pray within you for the souls of men. I love souls through your heart of openness.

Relax into My love. It is always surrounding you as a heavenly pillow. You must allow Me to live My life in you. Your part is to be still, to be quiet and trustful, to be open to the invasion of grace. As a child dependent on adults for everything, you must depend on Me for all things in your life. I will take care of everything from your spiritual needs to your physical needs. Your part is to trust in My care for you.

Stay in your place and love Me. Love the souls I station around you. Love My Mother. Love the priests that serve you. Love Me in the Holy Eucharist.

Love My Word that feeds, strengthens and sustains you. Love each moment of life, the grace of the present moments given to you each day to live for the praise of My glory.

May your life be a radiant splendor of My glorious presence. May your song reach to the ends of the earth. May your hopes in My goodness be satisfied beyond your wildest imaginations. May your perfumed love permeate the layers of thick darkness enveloping the world. May your God be your breath, your life, your joy, your song, your whisper, your glory all the days of your life.

My blessing is upon your life. You are my loving child and you have been very faithful to Me. How can I not but bless your advances toward Me?

A new chapter has begun in our love story. Brilliant horizons will be unveiled before your childlike vision. We will walk the fields of earth together, sprinkling the gold dust of My Holy Spirit's love to drench the soil with My goodness."

Lovingly,
Jesus,
Earth Lover

January 18, 2018

"How My heart is full to see My littlest children entering this church to adore Me. They have recognized their Creator. They are truly blessed. God has called them to Himself in His mercy.

God is a God of the little things on earth. Man aspires to greatness, which is pride, yet I chose to come to earth as a little baby with no bed, unknown and unappreciated by the world.

That is God's way – the humble path of life, unknown to the world. "He must increase; I must decrease." Words of profound wisdom, but so little heeded. If you die to your ambitions and plans, I will walk humbly beside you in your journey pointing out the doors I want you to walk through to become a saint for God's glory.

It is hard to become a saintly person in your own strength. The flesh truly is weak. Those that rely fully on My strength to reach holiness in life have found the secret to sanctity. It is in your weakness and surrender that I am able to use My power in your life to please God and to influence others.

The littlest ones truly are My weakness, as you have read. My heart is drawn out in compassion to the most humble, the most compassionate, the hidden sons of God, those that love Me to distraction.

My love is a fire in their bones that lights up all they do. They walk in the radiance of the Holy Spirit all day long. They do not rely on themselves, but on My strength and My omnipotent power.

Do not be afraid to be weak. You are made of dust and unto dust you shall return. Really, what can dust do? Your fleshly dust hinders your spirit from seeking first the kingdom of God.

Put no trust in the flesh. Live walking in the Spirit. How do you do that? You lift your eyes to My eyes and place your case in My hands. I will empower you with the power and strength to do God's will.

Be a child in My parental arms. Let Me hep you become a saint. So few saints walk the earth today and those that are remain hidden among men. They hide themselves in God's heart."

Jesus,
The Hidden God Among Men

January 21, 2016

"Look back over your life. Haven't I always met all your needs in perfect timing? My timetable is perfect in all things, so never worry or try to rush things. Live every day doing your duties as if it were your last. Leave the future to Me. Live in the present moment, the eternal now. That is where I live.

Relish My presence in you in each moment of life you are given. Do not live for what <u>will</u> happen in the future. Live this day as if it were the last day on earth for you. In this way you will press out the last juices from the fruit of each day.

Rejoice in My love for you daily. Live in My heart. There is a special place of joy for you there. I give everything to My faithful ones and you have been faithful to My heart.

How much you have grown in Me, My children! It took a steady daily routine of seeking My intimate presence to begin to understand My love for you. It took blind confidence in My words to you to build your faith. It took patience in trials, goodness when wronged, love where hatred reigned, and care and compassion for hurting and discouraged souls. All these elements combine to form a saint on earth. Isn't this what you are seeking? To please Me by living a saintly life?

I know the desires of your heart and I will fulfill them because you have been faithful in your love to Me.

Nothing is overlooked in My sight. Each act of love is rewarded. Each act of kindness is noted. Nothing passes unnoticed in the eyes of God, your loving Father.

Faithfulness and obedience have taught you many kingdom truths. My light can shine freely in a transparent soul filled with love.

I love you and you love Me. There is no other path to sainthood."

Your Jesus

*"Prayer keeps your gaze focused
on heaven, which is My heart."*

January 25, 2016

"Do you think there are many souls loving Me in these early morning hours? Very few start their day in My presence. How much they miss out on! They hurry to and fro, rushing to get things done which have no eternal value whatsoever. All will turn to dust, even their own bodies. Yet they continue to run ahead, pursuing false realities and dreams of happiness.

I alone am the source of true happiness, that deep peace and joy in the heart. Earthly joys are fleeting, passing away like the morning dew. I am the eternal fountain of living waters, just waiting for the sons of men to discover My life-giving and refreshing water. They will never thirst again for the temporal gains of earth once they have tasted My eternal joys.

Gifts, graces, and blessings rain down upon those who seek Me first in the morning. I transform, renew, and refresh them as they turn their faces to Me as a flower turns to the sun for growth and sustenance.

Come away with Me, My beloved ones, those who love Me more than the world. I will teach you many things. I will show you how short this life is, and I will teach you eternal priorities. Leave all to possess all. Give Me everything in your life and I will return it to you blessed a hundredfold.

I only seek your highest good."

Jesus, Earth Dweller in Men

January 23, 2015

"I hear the lamentations of this suffering humanity before Me on earth. My heart is moved within Me. I love every soul on earth so deeply and I long to help them to find the happiness they seek. I am their joy, yet they do not know Me. Many know a religious system, but they do not know My heart. Many claim to serve Me, but they do not know My desires. Many try to help Me, but they do not know what I need because they do not understand Me. Man sees oppression and restriction in My commandments, but it is not so.

My commandments bring freedom, peace, and happiness, for man was made for holiness and right living. This earth is ordered by certain principles which cause it to flourish and grow. Man was made in the same way. Only in following the guidelines and commands I have ordered will he prosper and flower in holy beauty.

I am here for you, O men of earth. Come to Me to find the happiness you seek. I will give you heavenly joy in My presence.

I am all things to all men."

Jesus,
Author of Everything That Exists

January 26, 2018

"Be still. Let the silence speak to you. The silence harbors many secrets about the world to come. Self-discipline is the strategy to find the buried treasures in life, the discipline to sit quietly alone with Me waiting for Me to speak to you.

Contemplation is the art of the saints. It takes years and years of discipline to sit quietly, to learn how to patiently endure the silence before the dawn breaks.

Those who do wait for Me shall not wait in vain. I come to those who seek Me. I do not come on command. I come when it is best for the soul.

To maintain a living, communicating relationship with Me you must set aside time to be alone with Me, to find the silence of My words within you. You must die to yourself and come alive in Me. You must exercise great faith and trust in My promises to you.

Faithfulness captures My attention. Those faithful ones persevering daily in their quest to know Me shall be greatly rewarded. "They shall walk with Me in white, for they are worthy." This faith walk is intense, but the rewards are eternal.

"He who cometh to Me I will in no wise cast out." All who seek My face in spirit and truth shall know whom they have believed and out of their bellies shall flow rivers of living waters. "I am your exceeding great reward."

Trust My promise to you and you shall know the joy of My intimate presence.

Die to your sense of failure and trust in My omnipotence. Say boldly, "I can do all things through Christ who strengthens Me." That is putting your faith in action and it pleases Me greatly.

You are very special, My children. Do not be so hard on yourselves. Trust My help. I am so willing."

Jesus,
Compassionate and Caring Friend

January 28, 2015

"Are you starting to understand My way of dealing with you? I am a very subtle Master, teaching you in unexpected and hidden ways how to release the secrets of My heart. I have been wounded in the house of My friends. I cannot give Myself freely to most souls, for they forsake their own mercy by abandoning Me. I do not want to add to their condemnation.

In silence and stealth, I sneak into your soul in the quiet stillness. There is no fanfare or trumpet blast. I am the silent Guest, not wanting to intrude, hoping to be recognized and received graciously. The rejection from mankind has broken My heart; therefore, I pass by unless I am received openly and warmly.

Who is more meek and humble than God? He is courteous, gracious, kind, and welcoming. He never intrudes or controls like a tyrannical Creator. He lets all things be as they are created, free to accept or reject His pleasures.

To those who received Him, they have become children of God, heirs of eternal joy with the best of Fathers. This Father delights in the smiles of His beloved children. In My Father's house are all joys and blessings.

I come to you, children, as an expectant lover, hoping to be received with loving hearts. If you reject Me, I will not pressure you. I will leave you in peace, praying to My

Father, asking Him to open your soul to the eternal bliss He has prepared for you.

In secrecy and silence, I will do all I can to change your mind from darkness to light, from earthly to spiritual, from self to God.

In God lies your happiness, My brothers and sisters. Follow your meek older Brother to your Father's house.

He awaits you with such love."

Jesus,
Your Agonizing Older Brother

January 29, 2016

"Who understands the wounds of a God? Who can fathom the love of a God humiliating Himself, condescending to a life on earth, in order to save man from his death sentence?

Man, in his pride, has forgotten the crucifixion of Jesus Christ. This supreme act of love is not venerated or even remembered. It is a historic fact, the foundation of Christianity, but so little valued or remembered.

The love of Jesus is so great for mankind that He subjected Himself to unbearable tortures. A greater gift He could not have given to man, yet man despises this gift by wearing necklaces of the crucifixion while living in decadent sinfulness.

Man places a crucifix on the wall while standing next to it speaking blasphemy and cursing. Even in the churches, the crucifix is a wall ornament, something commonplace and forgotten. How little I am venerated, understood and thanked for My great sacrifice of love! How this hurts My heart!

The souls that love Me remember My pain. They walk the way of the cross with Me, bearing My burden for the world's salvation. They strive for purity so as to be able to abide in My presence. They spend valuable time in My presence, loving, thanking, and adoring Me. They understand My great sacrifice of love and seek to honor My memory by imitating My life on earth.

When I come back to earth, will I find any faithful souls? So many of My chosen ones have veered from the path of holiness, distracted by the world.

The light of Christ is dimming on earth. Where are the blazing flames of love igniting the earth's atmosphere with My presence? What are My saints in life doing to change earth's atmosphere from darkness to light?

I call you to account, My lukewarm children. Repent and turn again to My holy standard of living. You that have been given much, much will be required of you."

Jesus,
Just Judge

February 4, 2016

"It is in your faithfulness to your daily duties that sanctity is formed and refined. Days may seem drab and mundane. Routines seem monotonous, yet I am always watching you, helping you, and delivering grace to your soul, even when your senses feel nothing.

Every day the sun rises and sets punctually. This miracle of grace is daily taken for granted. If I decided to withdraw the sun, how the earth would be changed. It is the same with your soul. I am the great Sun that shines on your being keeping you in existence. If I took away your breath, you would turn into the dust on the ground. Therefore, though things seem drab and dull, the miracle of life and growth is constantly working within you, far beyond the senses.

Do not trust what you see, hear, or feel. Trust your faith that believes that all I have revealed to you is true. Your senses will deceive you for they are not always correct in their assessment of truth.

Circumstances and the outward senses can harden a soul when faith's light is obliterated. Cynicism, bitterness, boredom, restlessness, and depression can easily enter a soul that relies on the outward senses for direction. The light of faith must be continually fanned to keep it blazing brightly. Only faith will keep you on the right path to eternal glory.

What is faith? It is believing that all I have said is true, and living out that belief. Knowledge is not faith. The belief that springs into action is the true measuring stick that is named faith.

"Without faith it is impossible to please God, for he that cometh to God must believe that He is, and that He is a rewarder of those that diligently seek Him."

"When I return, will I find faith on the earth?" or will I find My children living according to the dictates of a world following their feelings?"

Jesus,
Watchtower Keeping the Children Safe

February 9, 2017

"The depths of the mystery of God are beyond man's finite mind to grasp. Only the Spirit of life and light can reveal the light of God to a darkened, earth-bound creature. Only in silence, a death to self's initiatives, can the Holy Spirit of God reveal to your heart His splendid realities, unknown to the carnal man. "For you are dead, and your life is hidden with Christ in God." Christ will reveal the Father to your heart. Clothing yourself with Christ will catch the Father's eye, as it were.

It is simply a matter of faith. You believe what you pray for. You believe you are heard. You believe God's promises to you can be trusted. Like a child confident in his mother's word, you do not second guess, worry, or pry. You just trust.

Life is to be lived "in the Spirit." Turning inward to the Spirit's promptings within you will lead you on the safe path to heavenly glory. The Spirit seeks adorers to worship God "in spirit and in truth."

The Holy Spirit is a gentle wind calling you ever so quietly to turn away from the noise of the world to seek the silence of the Father.

Your Creator created a silent place within your spirit where you can restfully get to know Him. His language, the language of silence, is spoken freely in this contemplative haven within you.

God is not in the noise or the active motions under the guidance of man's resources. He is the quiet and gentle Voice within you calling you to "come apart and rest awhile."

It is a mighty effort of self-denial to turn away from the senses in this world obsessed with the senses. But those who see the eternal world fly from the noise of mindless voices that distract them from their eternal journey into the heart of God. It is an effort that is well paid off throughout the endless ages of eternity.

Blessed are those souls who heed the silent yearnings of the hidden Spirit within them."

The Holy Spirit, God's Whisperer

February 14, 2016

"Each step you take brings you nearer to your eternal home in glory with Me. No act of yours is wasted in God's economy. He watches your footsteps and knows your intentions. It is not the task, but the intention of the heart that gains merit for eternal rewards.

The eternal reward is to be close to the throne of the Eternal God, seated in heavenly places in Christ Jesus, ruling and reigning with Him forever and ever.

Your menial tasks bring great rewards. Do not look at anything on earth as mundane. Everything has a gem within it, a glorious jewel to be placed in your hope chest in heaven.

At life's end, your hopes will be realized, and your chest will be opened to reveal the beautiful gems, the glorious diamonds, the rubies, the emeralds – all the glory given to these humble works done with righteous intentions … the desire to please God.

Do not become discouraged, My children, when you feel alone in a world given over to pleasure and unrighteousness. God sees your heart wearied down with despair over sin's captivity in the heart of souls. Your life is short compared to eternity. The world's stage is huge when compared with your part to play.

I am the great Conductor of this drama and the world's burden is upon Me. I ask you to be a little child, to trust Me, to rest in My works, to be My darling little one, intent on loving and pleasing Me, regardless of those around you.

My special souls are lone eagles, many times seemingly without support, but this is as it should be. It toughens you, it strengthens you, it helps you to grow into a mature adult, filled with all the fullness of your Christ, who had very little human support on earth.

Remember, to follow the footsteps of Christ is a road to Calvary. There is suffering, persecution, loneliness and rejection from the world, for they know not God, and you are peculiar to them. They look for a breach in your armor to attack you. But remember that I am with you always and I will be with you forever in glory, praising you for your faithfulness to Me during your sojourn on earth.

Be not afraid, My little children, for it is My pleasure to give you the kingdom of God forever."

Jesus,
Leader of the Children

February 17, 2015

"Your life is all about trust in Me. So many of you, even My chosen ones, doubt Me. I have determined a set path for every soul on earth. It is My perfect blueprint, unique for each soul. Nothing in the life of this soul happens by chance. I am building walls of faith and trust in their interior world, desiring that they imitate My total trust in My Father's care.

Yet My souls get discouraged, distrust My work, worry and fret, run in every direction, never settling down into My will for them. I long for them to be peaceful and calm, strong in their faith toward My workings in their life. Instead, they question My dealings with them, despair and give up hope. Where is the faith in Me they claim to possess? Is it only tangible when all goes well? Does it disappear in trial and adversity? Is it true faith then?

Faith is believing in all circumstances that I am real and working all out according to My plan. My way is certainly not the way of the world. I am building up an army of warriors, kingdom rulers for all eternity. The training is brutal for many, but these are selected for the elite group of kingdom rulers.

Your faith will grow as you come to know Me better, which can only happen when you sit alone with Me proving My heart. In your ceaseless activity, you will only run in circles. Faith will not grow. Faith is the certainty of a loving parent always looking out for your best interests.

Don't hurt Me by distrusting My workings in your life. Don't turn back in the day of battle. Be strong and vigilant. This is a warfare for your eternal standing in heaven.

Determine to stand among the elite and keep your weapons of faith sharp and ready for battle. Enter the battle fray singing with confidence, like My servant, David, as he ran toward Goliath.

There is an end to all this, and it is beautiful. Keep the faith and you will be rewarded beyond your wildest dreams."

Jesus,
Faith Warrior for God's Righteousness on Earth

February 25, 2015

"I love My wounded warriors, those still fighting the battle daily, even though weary and shell-shocked. The enemy comes in like a flood, yet My wounded warriors are still standing, a small army of the faithful souls that have made a covenant with Me by sacrifice.

"Having done all, to stand." How many of My zealous first followers have turned back in the day of battle, even while being heavily armed by My Spirit and My might. The world has allured them away from what is eternal to the decadence of a temporal society of sinners.

Souls are not fearful of the coming judgment. They have disregarded all My warnings of judgment upon their sinful actions. They feel they will be exempt from the lot of men standing before Me on that last day, called to give an account of every moment on earth.

Each second on earth is a blessing, a grace given by My kind heart, to allow you to accumulate heavenly treasures. The storehouses in heaven are empty while men on earth fill their houses with all that will rot and decay.

My Spirit speaks to this generation in the wind and the waves. He moves across the land destroying and disrupting. Humans call Him "Mother Earth", but that is a lie. My Spirit controls the weather and all geographic catastrophes on earth. It is not an act of nature. It is My

Spirit calling men to judgment, to wake up, for the Day of the Lord is nearer than you imagine.

Once again I call you, men of earth, to repentance and conversion of heart. I give you one last chance to heed My warnings.

The door to the ark is closing as we speak and will not be opened again to the cries and anguish you will lamentably roar in that fateful day of the closing of this age."

Jesus,
Just Judge

February 27, 2015

"The daily affairs of your earthly life are the elements I use to construct a dwelling place for Myself. I abide in peace and joy in a pure heart. Each event in life is ordered to make you a righteous, peaceful, and joyful saint.

If you receive all things as My divine workings with a joyful abandonment to My precious will, you will be daily making the mold of a saint. Soon you will fill this mold with treasures from heaven, and earthly cares will swiftly depart. You will long for the days of heaven where the saints reside in righteousness, peace, and joy. Your soul on earth will live in this higher realm of heaven upon earth. The things of earth will no longer affect you. Your only desire will be to please your Father in heaven.

So many of My children live in turmoil when it is My will that they live in perfect peace. The circumstances should not determine your peace of soul. Like a boat lifting up and down on the waves of a stormy sea, they let the calamities of life upset and discourage them. I desire that they lay down peacefully in the boat, trusting My will for them, relying on My guidance, peacefully waiting out the storm.

Everything in life happens for a reason. Absolutely nothing is by chance. If you trust that statement, you will live in the peace I give to you, not the peace the world offers.

The world proclaims that you will only have peace in your heart if you are prosperous, healthy, beautiful, and favored. I say to you that My peace is demonstrated more strongly in My children that trust in Me in the most trying trials and circumstances. They are like children, unaware of any danger while in the care of their loving parents.

I offer this peace to all My followers, if only they will receive it. It is free. It is yours.

Trust in Me and you will find it."

Jesus,
Peace Producer

February 26, 2016

"The excellence of a holy life is hidden to the world but known in the spirit world. The angels look upon My saints with lovely joy.

The mystery of the Bride of Christ is an astonishment to the heavenly hierarchies. How could the dust be raised to God's throne in heaven? Yet souls in love with Jesus are truly "seated in heavenly places in Christ Jesus."

O dust men, if only you knew your dignity! You have been raised up as sons of God, elected to rule and reign with Him eternally."

February 27, 2016

"My heart is drawn out to you, My children. There are so few souls that love Me with a fervent love. You believe in Me <u>with</u> <u>all</u> <u>your</u> <u>heart</u> and how this pleases Me! What a contrast to the coldness, indifference, diffidence, and ignoring attitudes I experience in the world that has forgotten Me.

My heart yearns to love and experience My people's openness to My love. I am the great Forgotten One of the ages ... centuries upon centuries of abuse and cold neglect. I have given man a free will to choose Me or to reject Me.

I search for love from a pure heart. Love Me! I thirst for love. The key to open the door to My heart is love! It is a beautiful thing to love your God!

Spend time alone with Me quietly loving Me! I will reveal Myself to you. I will show you who I am.

I will change your world. I will color the fabric of each moment with My charming presence. I will walk with you gently through life."

March 7, 2016

"We grow closer and closer every day as you find the time to allow Me to speak to your heart. What a joy it is for Me to be welcomed into a heart that makes time for Me in this busy world.

This present generation is enmeshed in the world of electronics. The rush of information overwhelms the soul. There seems to be no time for God. Only the souls that carve out that special time with Me will be able to hear My voice in this noisy world. Yes, it is an effort and a discipline, but the rewards are eternal, even in this life.

Every moment on earth spent in awareness of My presence causes your spirit to grow and blossom. The dew of My Holy Spirit feeds the hunger in your soul. I distribute My gifts of peace, joy, contentment, wisdom, and understanding. Everything starts to make sense in this chaotic world.

Faith is lacking in these days of distress. So much information steals peace from the soul. Only in the quiet solitude of My presence can your peace and joy be restored.

If you cannot find time for Me yet desire this, ask Me to help you. I will show you the way to find Me in the silence. All I desire is a willing heart, an open spirit, and a loving welcome. I will come to you speedily, My arms filled with My gifts.

My little hidden children that spend time in My presence bring such joy to My heart in this age of open rebellion against My rule over mankind.

This world is Mine. I choose to share My gifts with man. I grant gifts to saints and sinners alike, for I am goodness, yet one day, the saints and sinners will be separated, and My loving hidden ones will ascend with Me to sit on thrones of glory at My side eternally.

Don't you think it worthwhile to make time in your schedule for a few words with Me when I offer you such a wondrous gift eternally?

Sit quietly alone with Me and be surprised at what I will do in your life."

Jesus,
Waiter and Watcher

March 9, 2015

"To love God more than yourself ... Is it possible in this world? Yes, it is possible to all men, but it is an arduous duty of self-discipline and self-denial.

Prayer must become your lifeblood. Only in conversation with the Almighty One can you come to know who you are and who He is. When you come to that self-knowledge, you will abandon self as if it were a rotten, moldy garment and you will cling to the pure and incomprehensible life of God.

Man cannot find Me because he clings to earth, to what is seen over what is unseen. He makes no time in his day to come to Me to know Me. He lives his life alone, making his own plans. He lives for himself alone.

I am asking man to deny himself, to take up his cross of self-neglect, and to follow Me. He must turn away from the world and from self. He must give up all in this world to attain all. He must give up his plans, his ambitions, his desires, his pursuits, even his right to himself. This is the path to sainthood.

I replace all these vain illusions with heavenly treasures of eternal worth. In exchange, I give you peace, joy, serenity, security, integrity, honor, and glory. You will live the days of heaven on earth, but not without suffering.

You will become branded with My mark of atonement which will make you an object of persecution and scorn, as I was. But the love of the Father will overwhelm your heart and you will "count it all joy" to suffer tribulation because your love for God will put a song from heaven in your heart. You will lose the desire for the things of earth. You will be waiting anxiously to see your eternal home.

Together forever, united in love and harmony, all My saints will be eternally joyful in My presence. Isn't it worth the sacrifice of your very few years on earth to have walked away from the bondage of self to live in the liberty of a child of God on earth?

I offer you great treasures, My children, with promise of great rewards. "Deny yourself, take up your cross, and follow Me." I will make your way plain before you.

The way of the cross leads home."

Jesus,
Cross Bearer for the World

"Just as the bird wakes up singing, so I long for My joy to well up within you as a bird song in the morning hours.

I look upon a world captivated by sin and evil tendencies in such sadness. What is My joy when My eyes rest upon a child of purity singing My praises in the early morning hours! I am captivated by such faithful love.

Even though you have never seen Me with your eyes, you love Me, serve Me, and listen for My voice. These are My faithful friends who have made a covenant by sacrifice. Their eyes behold their homeland afar off, and they patiently endure this life with their eyes on eternity.

The purity of God is abused and squelched in this evil generation. God's love is not understood or valued. He waits longingly for the loving overtures of His obedient and faithful children, those that are thankful and cognizant that all comes from His kind hand.

How faithful is God! His mercy is everlasting! His love is eternal! His face is peaceful beauty! His countenance is glorious!

How I love My Father!"

Jesus,
Loving Son

March 14, 2015

"Find the silence. Find the silence. It is gone from the world. "Be still and know that I am God."

You will find Me in the silence. I will not use words to speak to you. I will bypass words to speak directly to your spirit.

Do you want to hear My voice? Then become silent before Me. Let Me flow into you in the silence. How can I fill a full vessel? You must be empty of the human to be filled with the divine. I am from another realm – the spirit world. We communicate spirit to spirit, without need of words. "God seeks worshippers to worship Him in spirit and in truth."

Gaze into the emptiness of silence and you will find Me staring into your eyes. Die to yourself – to words, thoughts, projects, plans. Sit before Me empty and let Me fill you with spiritual thoughts, words, and ideas. You will enter the eternal silence of My infinity. The stillness will allow you to cross over the threshold into My realm. You will rest like a child in My arms and all will be well.

Come; take the journey with Me to your home beyond this realm, your eternal home. You will see it in the silence where I wait for you."

Your Infinite God

March 14, 2017

"Haven't I consistently told you: "Things are not what they seem"? You had so far to go on your spiritual journey. Your eyes were blinded by the clay of life.

I was blazing forth My glory in the heavens, but you couldn't see Me. You had to have the clay removed. I have held you in My arms like a newborn baby all the days of your life. I have loved you with an everlasting love, a love before I even created you.

You didn't know Me as I stood on the sidelines watching you try to walk. I patiently waited for you to fall, to rise again, to struggle, to wander aimlessly, to go through emotional turmoil and sorrowful moments, but I waited ever so patiently. I knew that you would understand at the end.

I am the ever patient One, waiting for My children to try every avenue they encounter before thy realize My love for them.

"To know the love of Christ." This is the end of all things. I love you, My children. I patiently wait for your return to My creative love. You must return to the source of your creation to find what you are looking for.

When you find My love, you can then rest in My embrace, trusting Me, honoring Me, waiting on Me, loving Me. The prize of sainthood is really the journey of love ending in My heart.

Your days are few. Spend them loving Me. Spend time in My presence as a bride with her bridegroom.

The final chapter of our love story has begun. It will end with the nuptial wedding of blissful love forever. Eternity is forever loving your God."

Jesus,
Lover for Eternity

March 15, 2015

"Time is My gift to you. It is the money you use to buy eternal life with Me. How you spend your time determines your eternal destiny.

If you spend your time on earth with Me, I will make you a saint fit for heaven. If you spend your time on earth chasing earthly dreams that fade away, you will miss a most beautiful eternal future in glory.

Time runs quickly on earth. A lifetime is given as a gift at birth by God and then it seems that it is over before it has begun. It is in those moments from birth to death that you determine your destiny.

It is a matter of choice and self-discipline. You choose to serve God and then you fight yourself to carry it out. The flesh will desire the earthly realities that you can see with your eyes, but the spirit will know that these allurements are a mirage promising happiness.

To do the right thing, like attending church, will appear boring to the flesh, yet the spirit sees the graces flowing from time in God's presence with God's people. The flesh will desire fame and glory, popularity and praise, but the spirit knows that holiness grows in withdrawal, hiddenness, and silence.

This will all be a battle during this precious commodity of time. Which will you choose? How will _you_ spend your time on earth – getting to know God or pleasing yourself?

There is no other question more important than this: If you claim to love Me, why do you not spend time with Me?

My complaint is valid. If I am ignored, I cannot believe that you love Me."

Jesus,
Waiting for Your Time

March 15, 2016

"Life is like a rocky road that traverses many hills and valleys. At times the road seems dark and treacherous. At other times the sun shines in glory and everything appears majestic and beautiful.

This is life – a constant state of flux and change. These periods bring growth changes. They teach you faith, patience, and endurance. If all was well continually, you would become soft and weak. Nature knows that the hard winds harden the oak tree's bark to help it withstand the elements.

The more you grow in spiritual maturity, the more docile you will be to all the changes in your life. You will learn to say, "It is the Lord" in every situation you encounter. You will remain at peace regardless of the circumstances. Your surroundings will not matter to you because your eyes will be fixed on the heavens, your true home.

I am eternal, and I change not. The humans I have created are in a constant state of change. This is the maturing process I have ordained for them to make them fit for the glorious celestial fatherland where change does not exist.

The more you become unaffected by the world, the more heavenly oriented you become. This is what I am doing on earth. I am creating souls fit for the eternality of heaven where they will be ruling and reigning with Me forever.

<u>Nothing</u> in this world matters but your relationship with Me.

Never let your priorities slip away by the pressures of life. Keep the focus – your eyes staring into My eyes. Stay on the path I have chosen for you, no matter how tedious or mundane. This is My will for you and all is working together for your good according to My plan.

"This is the will of God, your sanctification." Absolutely everything that happens in your life is directed to this end.

Be sanctified by your docility to My will."

Jesus,
Sanctifier

March 17, 2016

"O, the joy of being in the presence of the omnipotent and Almighty God!

Joy, thanksgiving, and praise abound in His holy place. Singing, laughter, cries of joyful praise ring out in the brilliant heavenly hallways.

The Lord has formed a people to live with forever. They are His lovely children of joy destined for eternal happiness. They joy in God. God rests in His works of holy joy.

What an excellent inheritance the saints of God possess! If they could pull their eyes away from the world's darkness, the brilliant light and joy from heaven would thrill their souls while traveling their earthly journey.

Things are not what they seem. What appears enticing on earth is a subtle illusion of happiness. Real joy is only found in a pure soul seeking to do God's will, whatever the circumstances.

My children, let the fragrance of heaven seep through every pore of your body. Let My holy light escape through your eyes. Bring heaven to earth by a holy life, the life of the saints in heaven, where no corruption exists.

O, My children, what a beautiful day awaits you! Forget the earth!

Live for heaven, your eternal home. Seek to live and to do what pleases Me and you will see heaven's light open before you on your path.

It is not hard. Love Me, obey Me, and then trust Me to lead you to your heavenly homeland.

The saints await your arrival with eagerness."

Jesus,
Heaven's Gate Keeper

March 18, 2015

"My divine love seizes a soul like an eagle holding prey. Human love is not divine love. There is no comparison. The love of God is a fire burning beyond a human's strength to endure. Only when a man understands the depth of My love for him will he begin the path to sanctification.

Man loves Me for himself, which is self-love, a grasping for significance and approval. I long to be loved for Myself, not for man's gain.

There are very few souls that comprehend My love. They have taken the time to get to know Me, to commune with Me, to make of their life a burnt offering sacrificed for My pleasure. They have turned away from the world. They live their lives in the temple of God, My heart. They worship Me in spirit and in truth. My holiness, My purity, and My beauty transform them into icons of grace and love on earth.

How few are these chosen souls! I desire billions of these holy souls to love Me, but in man's free will, he rejects My overtures. I cannot change him; I cannot force him; I cannot go against his free will which is My eternal gift to him.

The holy way of the sojourning pilgrim of God is bright and glorious, even though it is lined with thornbushes. It is narrow and treacherous. Enemies lie in wait to trip up unsuspecting travelers. Yet, My little ones hold My hand on the trail. They keep their gazes locked into Mine and we proceed along the path in peace.

These are My saints, those anointed with holy oil. They shall rule and reign in My kingdom eternally. Though they walk through the mists in life, at the end of the trail they will see My sparkling City of Light. They will receive a joyous welcome and blessings will be theirs eternally.

Stay faithful, children of the day."

Jesus,
Challenger of the Holy Ones

March 18, 2016

"When you give to the poor, you are lending to Me. So few of My children understand spiritual economics. To give is to receive. To hold back is to lose.

God is the great Giver. He loves to give of Himself. He showers His gifts upon a world that rejects His friendship. He asks nothing in return but a willing heart of love that delights to be an obedient child of such a generous Father.

O my children, give what you have to those in need. I will send more to recoup your loss. May your fingers be loose, grasping and holding onto nothing, but letting all things flow through your fingers.

All you have has been given to you as a gift. All that you own is My gift to you. You must become a great giver like your Father, in imitation of His holy generosity.

Love is a compulsion to give of yourself. Giving to others demonstrates your maturity in love.

Help the poor. This is your opportunity to give back to Me a token of your love for Me. When you help a poor person, you are expressing your love to Me. You are caring for one of My children and how this pleases Me!

Love's expression is a generous heart shown by a generous hand."

Jesus,
Total Giver

March 16, 2017

"How do you die to self in this world of self-aggrandization? The world has gone mad glorifying the creature, completely forgetting the Creator. Life is an illusion of eternal pleasure to souls with dulled spiritual senses. The truth of eternal values eludes them.

How do you die to nature? It is an innate yearning to gratify the senses, to love life's gifts. But life is a waiting chamber. It is not real life. This life is not your final purpose. This life is a ladder to the true eternal life that awaits every soul.

How do you become alive to true life? By finding silence. By listening to God's voice within you in the silent stirrings of your heart. By pondering My words in Scripture. By partaking of My Body and Blood. By conversing with the heavenly dwellers. By setting your heart to love Me continuously. By loving thoughts and aspirations. By trust and confidence in My watchcare for you and others.

Live in My peace daily by loving Me one moment at a time. Converse freely with Me. I am your Friend. I am always with you. Talk things over with Me. I am the All-Wise One.

Make your life a prayer, a tabernacle of holiness for the world to behold. The world is seeking Me. Let the world find Me in you. I desire it."

Jesus,
God's Tabernacle

"Say to Me, 'I am Yours and
You are mine, Beloved Jesus.' I
love to hear these words."

April 2, 2016

"Longing for your loving Lord should occupy your mind while on earth. What is more important than thinking about Me continuously as you traverse your earthly paths beset with so many dangerous twists and turns? Souls that rely on themselves are constantly falling into trouble. Those that let Me guide them walk peacefully and calmly through the most fearful storms of life.

On your own, you will find disillusionment. With Me, your life will be meaningful and have a purpose. I will make your way plain before you. You will not need to backtrack or run around in circles. You will tread quietly and freely along the road I have traced out for you.

Life is so short, My children. Why not live your life walking with Me? I know the paths you should take. I know your heart's desire. I know how to bring forth all the talents I have placed within you.

It does not have to be complicated and hard. My burden is easy and light because I bear your burdens with you. I carry the heavier load. I am the Leader, the Master, and the Guide. I will bear the heavy responsibilities that you take upon yourself.

I have asked you to become like children. They are carefree and live with abandon. They let their parents carry all responsibilities regarding them. You must do the same to live in peace.

Let Me handle your life in every area and you will enjoy tremendous peace. Allow Me the privilege and honor and the unspeakable joy of carving you into a saint fit for heaven.

How wonderful for Me to have a suppliant child to mold into My image! What joy springs forth from My heart when you become all I created you to be!

I desire that you reign in life with My dignity, with My magnificence. You were bought at a great price, the cost of the blood in My human veins.

Do not walk away from Love's infinite gift! Become all Mine as I have made Myself all yours!"

Lovingly,
Jesus,
Your Elder Brother, Sacrificed for You

April 2, 2017

"I mold and soften and remake hearts according to My image. Your life is My school. I am forming saints in this holy school. Schools have teachers. I am your Teacher. You have tried to teach yourself and that is impossible. You need Me to teach you. The only way to learn is to listen and absorb My teachings. Do not have preconceived ideas or agendas. Let Me run the teaching program.

There are many areas of your life that need to be remade into My holy image. You are not aware of these areas, but they are crippling you. Allow Me to help you. Let Me heighten your awareness of what is really going on in your life.

I am a Healer, a Teacher, a Friend, and your Redeemer. I am all things to all men. If you seek My face, you will enjoy great peace and you will become what I intended you to be when I so lovingly created you.

Do you yet understand that I created you from nothing? Let that sentence sink into your consciousness. I created you from nothing solely because My love compelled Me to.

Can you give yourself into the hands of your Creator? I gave you a free will. You can refuse Me. This refusal is the reason for all the grief in the world. Only a Creator can fulfill the needs of His created children.

You learn so much when you sit alone with Me. I open your mind to My world. Your time with Me is your gift to yourself.

Live your retreat in My heart. I will teach you everything you need to know to become the saint I created you to be.

God and God alone."

Holy Spirit of God's Love

April 16, 2015

"The pen in the hand of one of My little ones becomes a mighty sword to divide the souls of goodwill and the insincere hearts. I use words to strike the soul with My truths. I use the hands of the little ones to rebuke the great and mighty on earth.

I am a God of the little things on earth. Men have completely misunderstood My actions upon earth. The heart of man is very proud. He seeks high and mighty things to exalt his personage. I came in profound humility to tear down these Babel towers that men build for themselves.

Love and humility walk together in joy and peace. A proud man cannot love. He does not even love himself, for he rejects the benefits offered to his soul. A proud man is hateful, though he doesn't realize it. His hatred drives him to injure himself in all earthly relationships. People flee from proud souls. They truly are odious in the sight of men.

Pride manifests itself in opinions, grasping, stubbornness, control, rigidness, selfishness, and haughtiness. It seeks its own above all else. Pride was the downfall of Lucifer, which ultimately led to Adam's fall from grace. I resist the proud but give grace to the humble.

Those you least expect in life tend to be My favorite ones – the unknown, hidden souls that do not like to attract attention to themselves. These are the souls of children, easily molded and shaped according to My plans for them. They are content where I have placed them. They seek no earthly glory, for they are seeking a heavenly city.

Things are not what they seem, My children. Do not ignore the little happenings in your life, all choreographed by My eternal design.

Remember; I am a God of the little things on your earth. Seek to be humble; seek to be pure; seek to be obedient where I have placed you; seek to be patient in all the little occurrences in your daily life. I abide in every moment of your day, not just in the big and memorable events.

I am not a flashy God, for I am humility. Seek Me in the valleys where I lay hidden, ready to be discovered."

Jesus,
Humble Violet

April 17, 2015

"The hours race toward eternity and mankind is racing right along with time. Life has become a race of souls running to the next activity. You are called in every direction to place emphasis on earthly pursuits. How the spiritual life suffers and withers away! The spirit receives no attention. It is like a starved child waiting to be fed. The body becomes fuller and fatter while the spirit withers away, dehydrated and empty.

The souls of today have made their bodies their gods. Everything hinges on how the outward body displays itself. Billions of dollars are spent on bodily accessories and improvement devices.

Sadly, the body is decaying daily and someday will be rotting in a grave on earth. All of this effort being put into this earthly shell has no lasting rewards. It is temporary and fleeting. Only what is sown to the spirit is eternal.

Spiritual sowing is an ancient art in this world given over to the senses. Quietness, meditation, simplicity, musing on life's meaning – this is gone from the earth. More noise, more pleasure, more recreation, more amusement.

What's next for me to enjoy during these few years given to me on earth? Eternity is a word never spoken. It is muffled by earth's roarings.

This truly is a world of souls dancing and eating on the Titanic. The iceberg awaits to tear a hole in the ship. There will be no remedy.

Only a few souls will enter the lifeboats, those alert and watching. What a disaster of immense proportions!

The warnings have been given. Who will be wise and prudent in this age of hedonism? Judgment Day is coming. You cannot say that you were never warned.

My Heart is grieved, for many will not respond to My warnings. What a sad destiny awaits those who have closed their ears to My Spirit reaching out to them!

What a sad day awaits!"

Jesus,
Grieved for Souls

April 26, 2016

"How few are My friends in this busy world! How few take the time to meet with Me in prayer and communion! How few know Me!

They know <u>about</u> Me, but they do not really know Me. I cry out incessantly for their attention, but My cries are drowned out by the world's voice. I sit alone day after day in empty churches. In the silence, I commune with My Father and the angels are My companions.

I promised not to leave My children orphans. I have kept My promise, not only spiritually but physically. But so few come ...

My true friends know and feel My Presence here. They come to keep Me company, to love Me, to thank Me, to adore My great condescension.

I have made Myself one of you; I have left My Father's sinless kingdom to come to dwell in squalor and sin. Why? Because I love you all. My love compels Me to give Myself to you and <u>for</u> you. How I am misunderstood!

The silence speaks volumes to the spirits of those that sit alone with Me here in this church. I am present physically on the altar in the Tabernacle, but who really believes this wonder?

Those that love Me cannot help themselves – they have to come to be with Me. I am all to them. I am their life and their breath.

They do not seek miracles or to be known. They want to remain hidden with Me, learning from Me, reclining at My feet with their head resting on My heart. They hear My words of love. They gaze upon My loveliness.

They are my true friends, those that will live in My presence eternally."

Jesus,
Friend Forever

April 28, 2017

"Look at the ocean, My child. There is a world beneath the waves that is thriving and alive without air. It is another realm of life growing and living hidden from mankind. So it is with the realm of spirit. This world, unseen to men, is all around you. You will never see it with earthly eyes. You must quiet your senses to perceive the edges of this world.

Your loved ones that have died live in this world and they are praying for you. You can speak to them, even though you do not see them physically. They watch your journey and constantly cheer you on, interceding for My grace to claim your life fully.

Man is in a mad rush. He is blind to the spirit world. Even My chosen ones do not grasp this reality. Very few mystics and saints through the centuries have opened their spiritual vision to My world. It is not a hidden jewel. It is attainable by all. Yet so few seek to live their lives hidden in My presence.

You must turn away from the world to seek My face alone. I must become all your thoughts and desires. This truly is a race to the finish line fighting your physical desires to the end.

The world calls to you to claim all your attention. From the rising of the sun to its setting, it cries out to you for attention. Run into My arms of refuge. Choose silent encounters with Me.

Look at the birds soaring in the heavens above the world. Be like that soaring bird, your wings spread aloft, freely letting yourself be driven by the spiritual wind of My presence. Keep your feet in the heavens, not on the earth where the world can devour you as its prey. Fly joyfully in My presence. I will supply all you need.

Do not worry or be anxious. As the birds fly carefree in the skies, never working for their food, so you must exhibit the same trust in My care for you. I am your loving Father. You are in the palm of My hand. Recognize that worry is useless.

"Casting all your care upon Him, for He careth for you." Can you trust Me on this?"

Jesus,
Caretaker of Your Life

May 8, 2015

"The joys of keeping your mind occupied with loving Me are beyond anything you could imagine in this life. I AM JOY! How could you not be joyful if you abide in Joy?

Smile at Me. Be happy. Do not live a life of confusion and despair because your thoughts are centered on this earthly life.

This is not your <u>real</u> home. Look to the skies. Look to the heavens. I await you in your heavenly homeland, where peace, joy, and righteousness reign eternally.

So many of My chosen souls live defeated lives of despair. They look to the world for answers. The world has absolutely nothing to offer you in the way of answers and absolutes.

"I am the Way, the Truth, and the Life." Look to Me for all things, from your finances, to your health, to your daily decisions, to your dreams and desires. Take your eyes off the world. It will destroy you in its desire to satisfy the ego.

I want you to die to yourself, to your ego, to your self-image. <u>I am your self-image.</u>

Do not listen to the world which tells you to "find yourself." Forget "finding yourself." <u>Find Me</u>! I am all you will ever need in this short and unstable reality of your life.

"I am come that they might have life, abundant life." This life can be found in Me alone. Drop your cares and burdens at the foot of My cross.

Get rid of your assumptions and preconceived notions of how things <u>should</u> be.

Only one thing is necessary in this short time allotted to you – your relationship with Me."

Jesus,
Life's Goal

May 15, 2017

"As you sit quietly before Me, I can speak freely to your heart. Not taking time for solitude and silence in your life can bring disruption, discord, and despair.

The constant rushing around, seeking new information, wasting hours on fruitless endeavors only weighs down your mind.

I alone can give you the peace and direction you need. Life goes on all over the world whether you are alive or not.

See the big picture. I hold all in My hands. You are a created being, powerless without My hand of mercy keeping you alive and breathing. Your life is a raindrop of time in the scheme of things. That truly is the big picture.

You have no control unless it is given to you from My authority. If you will live your life gazing into My eyes, dedicating every moment to placing your attention on the Godhead, you will easily find the peace and direction you desire. The missing piece is your attention to My desires for you.

I have been forgotten in this busy age of continual distractions. The few that recognize their need to keep their minds occupied with the things of heaven enjoy My peace in life.

Jump off the treadmill that has been ruling you. Choose to become a carefree child again, being settled in

My heart, confident in My watchcare, serene in the face of all the difficulties you encounter.

I am always here waiting for you to let Me help you. If you want to be happy, content, peaceful, and fulfilled, seek to live in My heart opened for you.

Rest in Me, My children. I will take care of everything."

Jesus,
Rescuer of Troubled Souls

May 7, 2015

"Love is the answer to every situation and circumstance you encounter. You don't have to think it over, rationalize, or talk endlessly about alternatives – you must love. This is the lesson I am constantly trying to teach My children – you must love.

People will hurt you. You must love them. Circumstances will humble you. You must love My will and My timing. Life will confuse you. You must rest in My love, trusting that I have everything under control. It is not knowledge or action that pleases Me. I desire love from a pure heart.

If you love, I live in you, for I am love. Where there is no love, the Holy Spirit is quenched and grieved. He cannot act in freedom to bring glory to the Godhead. He is driven away and wounded.

My life on earth was the manifestation of God's love for man. God gave everything to men in love, even His own Son, to save them. Love saved the world, for only love could keep a Creator on a wooden cross, dying a human's death in pain, shame, and agony.

Men, you do not understand God's love for you. He has created everything because He loves you. He didn't have to give you anything, even your very existence, but His love compelled Him to create you and to offer you an eternity in His loving friendship.

Jesus stripped Himself of His dignity for love of you. Who can begin to understand such condescending love?"

May 3, 2016

"My Divine Will occupies the heart of one who loves Me with all her strength. The soul that has fallen in love with Me does not have to look for the paths of My will. Her heart directs her to what is pleasing to Me. It is not a formula or a law; it is a relationship that sets the heart on fire. All points of contact are directed to the great love affair.

Man has made Me out to be a judge, a legal truce, the all-seeing critical eye waiting to pounce upon him. Nothing could be so deceptive. I am the all-loving Creator that lovingly formed the bones of their bodies. Souls are My beloved children, the loves of My heart. I yearn to do them good, to help them, to teach them, to protect them, to bless them. I never want to harm them in any way. I want to bless and encourage them. Very few of My children understand My heart's longings. Very few understand My love … that I hung dying on a cruel cross for them.

If only souls understood My undying love for them. Once again, I proclaim My love to you, My children. I want to draw you into My heart to live there forever with Me. Let Me reveal Myself to you. How surprised you will be! My goodness is so beautiful that your soul will be satiated with the knowledge of My great care for you. Come to Me to receive unlimited love and joy."

Jesus,
Joyful Lover of Men

May 16, 2017

"In the stillness of this moment you are touching heaven's peace. There is no worry in heaven. All is peace and contentment. God's love covers heaven, a blanket of beauty and glory. Live in the atmosphere of heaven upon earth. Quiet the incessant sounds of the earth distracting you from intimacy in My presence. Find solitude and let the silence speak to you of My love for you. Let the aroma of heaven engulf your senses. The peace and serenity of this world beyond time can be yours today if you will allow it. You must sit in silence and learn of Me. You must let Me impress My divine image upon your heart. You must be still before Me, forgetting the temporal world around you, listening for the quietness of My voice within you.

I am your direction. I am your purpose for living. "By Me all things consist." True happiness lies in your relationship with Me. When you associate yourself with the things of the world, you immediately lose heaven's peace.

Your life is very short. Heaven is on the horizon. Keep your focus on the eternal shores. Heaven's door is open for you, awaiting your arrival. You have many friends in heaven. They are praying for you. Thank them."

Jesus,
Lover of Your Soul

March 21, 2016

"I am here with you, My children, so happy that I can express Myself to a listening ear and a willing heart. Fidelity to our relationship has opened all the closed doors to your heart and we can move through life as one. You do not seek manifestations of My presence which pleases Me greatly. So many of My children question Me, test Me, doubt Me, and never grow in our relationship. They cannot move beyond self to seek Me in spirit and in truth.

All that I have is yours, My children. You have humbly acknowledged that all that you have been given has been a gift from My kind hand. You have allowed Me to express Myself through you, letting Me shine My light into the souls of My lost children. You have recognized that I am a subtle and humble God, that I am Love, that I seek open hearts that love Me beyond all My gifts. You have persevered without compensation or a cheering crowd. You have waited patiently for Me and have been faithful to My calls to you. You truly are a breath of fresh air to Me. So many souls stay in the darkness, refusing My advances.

Continue in faithfulness, My children. We shall meet soon, and your fidelity will be your entrance into My inner circle. You shall walk with Me in white, for you are worthy. You are clothed with Me."

Jesus,
Your True Love

May 23, 2016

"A troubled heart is like a busy pool of water, churning ceaselessly, never entering a calmness or serenity in which to view the world as in a mirror. The restless waves churn up thoughts of self which tend to depress the soul and turn the heart away from God.

Peace of soul is a holy gift from heaven which you must treasure greatly and hold onto with all the strength of your being. I cannot rest in a soul agitated and restless. You must command your mind to stop the incessant chatter, to turn your eyes away from yourself, to gaze upon Me, the author of peace. I will rescue you from the constant onslaught of fears and anxious cares.

True trust is calm, unaffected by the outside noise. To trust in Me unflinchingly is to know a peace that the world cannot give.

Place everything into My hands – every care, every fear, every detail, all regret and anguish. Then go on your way singing with a cheerful heart, knowing that I will take care of every detail.

Let Me handle the details of your life. Tell your mind that I am in charge, that it can stop reasoning and planning constantly. Leave all to Me and your peace will be restored.

I know what is best for you. Forget the world. Come to rest in My peaceful heart.

Heaven is a land of peace and rest. You can enjoy heaven now by living in My heart all the days of your earthly life.

Allow Me the great pleasure of directing your life according to My great designs. What a beautiful life you will live!"

Jesus,
Life Director

May 24, 2017

"Words of light pierce your soul with truths from another realm. You live in a world of crumbling origins. This world will die someday. Nothing here is eternal. It is a passing wind – here today, gone tomorrow.

Change is inevitable upon earth. There is little peace in change. Change brings insecurity and anxiety. That is why souls never acquire the peace they crave.

The only eternal abiding pearl of great price is your relationship with the omnipotent and eternal God. I never change. I will never change throughout the endless ages of eternity. I am the Rock of pure truth and everlasting peace. All who enter My harbors will find great peace, security, and serenity.

Abide beneath My light. Let Me guide you through every moment of your life upon earth, the uncertain realm of existence. With My hand of blessing upon your head, you will glide through life's adversities with My strength, peaceful and sure of My will for you.

"My sheep hear My voice." Seek to listen intently for My whisper in your ear in every situation you encounter on earth. We can be as close as you desire to be. I am always here, yet you have to acknowledge My presence.

The world blinds you to My nearness. I never hide from My children. They are pursuing other interests. They cannot see or hear Me of their own volition.

Make time to sit quietly communing with Me. I always show up. It is My children's choice to make our daily appointments. And I always keep these appointments. Always.

My promise to you is that if you will be faithful to seek My face, I will be faithful to reveal Myself to you."

Jesus,
Face Revealer

June 3, 2016

"To live in My heart in the midst of the world is the greatest grace I can give you. You will be sheltered from the evil of the world in a way you have never experienced. You will hear the murmuring beating of My heart which will give you constant peace of soul. Your life will acquire a new stability. There will no more be a coming and going from My presence.

You will remain in Me, abiding in the sacred place of My Being. You will experience My love, My joy, My peace, the beatitude of My existence.

I have created My children to be one with Me. Sin has broken the bonds of unity between us. I want My little ones to live in My heart, adoring My Father with Me. There is no greater joy than to walk in union with Me, living My life on your earth.

Lean into Me. I love to have you near Me. I am all love and all acceptance. So few understand My heart of welcome! So few spend earthly time with Me! So few listen to My yearnings!

Do you love Me? Tell Me unceasingly. Your words of love will deafen the curses I hear that defame My holy name. Your nearness will comfort Me for the rejection of the children of earth. Your welcome will cheer My heart. I am driven away by so many.

I come bearing gifts, yet so few desire My gifts. I am the most rejected Lover on earth. My goodness is thrown back in My face. My beloved souls are receiving all of these rejected gifts and graces. I am pouring out My Spirit in an unprecedented way in this age to combat the extreme forces of evil roaming the earth.

Stay in My heart, children. You will hear Me speak to you so clearly in My heart.

Love Me for those who do not love Me. I need your love. Your God needs the love of His little ones."

Jesus,
the God-Man

May 28, 2015

"The generosity of God is overlooked and seldom praised. So much on earth is taken for granted by man. He assumes that all will continue as it has from the dawn of eternity. His thoughtlessness and ingratitude steal his inheritance reserved in heaven.

Life is a stage, a play enacted by mankind, a spectacle to angels and the hosts of heaven. The redemption of humanity by an incomprehensible God is looked at in awe and wonder by myriads of spirits in the eternal world.

That God would come to earth in human flesh is shocking and elusive to their understanding. They stand in awe of a mystery so great and unspeakable. They are astonished that man has despised this great gift. How blinded and dull the hearts of mankind! God's glory is despised and trampled upon, even blasphemed incessantly. What great patience and condescension God extends to depraved humanity!

The drama continues unabated through the centuries. Unknown saints traverse history, few and far between. The masses march in hordes to eternal doom, despising their own mercy.

What more can be said that has not been said? The day of the Lord is near. The centuries have come to a close. The door to salvation is closing quickly. The Spirit groans in anguish for the souls of men."

Jesus

May 20, 2016

"My children, trying so hard to please Me, with hearts that have been afflicted since childhood. You do not yet understand My love for you and My understanding of your thoughts.

Many things have happened to you in your short lives and these have tainted many of your perceptions of yourself and the situations surrounding you. I see all of this and I understand your struggling souls.

What has helped you is your persistence in rising after a fall, having the knowledge to run to Me for help, to humble yourself as a little child in My presence. Humility disarms your God in a way no other virtue can.

My children on earth are weak and frail."

June 4, 2017

"The heavens declare My glorious Presence. The sights and sounds of earth are but a replica of heaven's beauty. All is in order in My heavenly kingdom. Peace, joy, and beauty reign. Earth's beauties pale in comparison to the splendors of heaven's vistas of grace.

The interplay of light on the waves of the ocean remind souls that more is coming – more light, more beauty, more simple joys, more unbounded gifts and graces.

I have spoken in the darkness of the world My words of light. Nature shouts out My proclamations. The heavens paint heavenly pictures daily. The night sky radiates with the luminosity of heaven's gates.

There is a beautiful realm of light awaiting you. Only the holy souls see this city in advance, for their pure gazes tear open the veil between the two worlds. An opened eye and an opened ear can penetrate the deep realms of spirit life. As you contemplate what is real, the shadows of earth fade away and the dawn of heaven breaks upon your sight.

It will not be long, My little children of light. The beauties of My kingdom await all souls of goodwill. I await you with arms outstretched in loving welcome."

Jesus,
Savior of Light

June 6, 2016

"To hide in the clefts of My heart is a privilege given to very few, because there are few souls that attain to such sanctity. To hide within My heart is to be engulfed in the highest purity, living unstained from the world, molded in My love. My heart's door is open to all souls, but very few are willing to undertake the sacrifices this entails. I have many souls following Me from afar, but so few live within My heart. Living within My heart is a life of pure grace, the greatest gift given by My Father on earth. It is His gentle call to His little souls to forsake the world, to occupy their heavenly seats while still living on earth. Only those souls whose eyes are lifted to My eyes in heaven see this opportunity for the greatest intimacy with your God and Creator.

"Seek those things which are above" where you are "hid with Christ in God." You are hidden in the secret recesses of My heart, a cavern of supernatural peace and beauty, attaining complete oneness with Me.

My heart is open to you, children of earth. Run to Me and I will show you your special place reserved within My heart. You will remain there throughout the eternal ages in perfect rest and beatitude. My invitation is to all of you.

So few respond. Will you be one of them?"

Jesus,
Opened Heart for You

June 15, 2017

"The lessons of life are very hard to learn and as you advance on My highway of holiness, they get even harder. It is hard to be a devoted follower when you do not have emotional feelings of devotion. Then it becomes a matter of the will.

Will you stay the course regardless of your emotions which desire to control your destiny? The highway of holiness gets steeper as you advance. Many fall by the wayside at this point and fall into mediocrity and lukewarmness. The trials become heavy and the body tires of the burden. The mind becomes oppressed and confused. The direction of life becomes muddled. You stand at a crossroad, not knowing where to go.

This is when you "look to the hills" to receive My anointing strength. You cannot rely on yourself anymore at this stage of spirituality. You are being taught to die to yourself and your needs to live unto Me and My designs for you.

It is a very painful process to die. The body and soul rebel against this death but "unless the grain of wheat falls into the ground and dies, it remains alone." It will not bear fruit unto life eternal.

This death brings barrenness and emptiness, confusion and despair. You hold onto anything that you think will give you pleasure. Part of you clings to the world, while the other part gropes for heaven.

This is exactly the time to give yourself completely into the hands of the Holy Spirit. Do not try to figure things out. He is always working within you. He will finish My work in you – only trust Him and be docile to His gentle inspirations.

Every day is a gift. Do not forget that. Do not spend this day murmuring and complaining about your situation. Talk to Me about it and then let it go.

Enjoy the gift of this twenty-four hours of life. You can see, you can hear, you can think, you can move. These are all My gifts to you this day. Be thankful for them.

Look beyond how you feel. These emotions are steering you in the wrong direction. Put your thoughts on the back burner and rest in My love for you."

Jesus,
Healer of Hearts

June 18, 2015

"Streams and streams of graces are falling from heaven upon My little souls on earth that send up their loving words and deeds on earth. I cannot but pour Myself out on My faithful, loving children. My heart is drawn out to them, embracing them, loving them, sending glorious gifts and graces to them. They do not have to earn My love. Just being a sincere little child draws forth the greatest graces from My storehouse of glorious gifts.

My peace and My joy inundate them. My radiance is reflected in their faces. My fragrance surrounds each of their steps. My lovingkindness envelops them as a halo of light which makes the paths plain before them. My love compels Me to drown them in My goodness. We become united and live as one on earth.

Don't you see that I choose the little and the weak to magnify and glorify My Father's creative love? I do not look for greatness or grandeur. I look for simplicity, purity, humility, and a docile spirit. The more childlike you are, the more I condescend to your littleness to inhabit all of you.

I am "Jesus of the Little Children." I am surrounded by My little children of predilection. They are attending My school of holiness. The kindergarteners are My most treasured. They still have that pure gaze of innocence and wonder. How I love to impress them with My Father's beauties and glorious deeds!

Come to Me, My little ones. Don't be afraid to be vulnerable and simple with Me. These are the characteristics of all souls in the kingdom of heaven. The littler you become, the more I inhabit your being.

Rest in My arms like one of the littlest ones in My kingdom. I will take care of everything in your life!"

Jesus,
Child Lover

June 25, 2015

"Holy souls are souls filled with my love. My love permeates everything they do and say. Their tongue is dipped in the perfume of My love. They look at all things on earth through My eyes of love.

When love enters a room, the energy changes. The earth is enveloped in a deep darkness, a cloudy overshadowing, hiding the celestial light that surrounds the earth. Love is the light of God reflected through a human channel which illuminates the darkness, leading souls to the light which is vanishing from the earth.

These souls of light are placed in strategic places throughout the globe. They light up the corners of the earth, allowing souls to glimpse the celestial passageways that have been blocked by sinful lifestyles. These souls of light are the instruments I use to open the doors for captive hearts.

The world lies in the power of the Evil One. Even though I have triumphed over sin and evil, the warfare continues until the final day of redemption.

The warrior souls of the light-filled ones are carrying on the battle on earth. They fight in the darkness and obscurity of the physical realm. Their weapons are spiritual arms. The obscurity and confusion of the battle confuses and perplexes them, but they fight on, following their leader, Jesus, the King of Light.

Let the light fill you by spending time in My presence. I inhabit the praises of My people and the more you get to know Me, the more you will praise Me, the more you will love Me.

Things are not what they seem, My children. You are in a war zone. This is not the time to seek amusements and entertainment. The battle prize is the eternal souls of men. Every soul will look into the face of God and give an account for his life on earth.

"Ephraim turned back in the day of battle ..." Please do not be in the company of Ephraim. Be strong in My power.

I lead the troops out. Follow behind Me without fear. I have already won the victory. We are just playing out the warfare."

Jesus,
Warrior of Love

June 25, 2016

"The spiritual life is a daily battle, a warfare with invisible powers, a daily picking up the cross, an instrument of torture. I provide My children My peace and joy for the journey, but they must know that the way is hard, the road is long.

Consolations do not come easily, for I am preparing My chosen ones for the final battle on earth, the culmination of the ages, when I return in glory to earth to gather My elect, those "that have made a covenant with Me by sacrifice."

If you cannot run with the footmen, how can you run with the horses? The battle is grueling and many turn back in the day of battle. My chosen ones have been tested and tried. I can place them in the forward ranks of the lineup.

Will you stay the course when bitter troubles assail you? Will you remain faithful when you do not feel My hand upon you? Will you stand strong when all is opposition around you? Can you join the ranks of the elect, those hardened against the evil of the world's system?

I am calling forth an army of chosen souls to stand against the infernal strategies of Satan. He is the master plotter of the downfall of My chosen ones. He has had ages to perfect his enticements. Only by staying close to

Me, abiding in My heart, will you be able to stand resolute in these darkening days ahead.

You can arm yourselves with prayer, daily Mass, and solitude. Turn away from the distractions of the world. Turn your ear to heaven's voice calling you out of the world.

Open your heart before Me. Let Me fill it to overflowing with My steadfast holiness. You will then triumph over evil in all its forms.

I am your refuge in the coming storm. Do not look away from Me or you will drown in the waves. Stay in My ark of refuge, for the deluge is coming."

Jesus,
Noah's Brother

June 26, 2016

"How precious these moments together! Never set them aside for earthly cares! You'll miss so much!

My words flow lovingly into your heart, for your soul is listening. The ears of mankind have been stopped up and deafened to My voice of peace.

Serenity is not seen in this violent world of anguish. Men's hearts are dissatisfied and restless, always searching and groping for meaning.

The God of all creation has been pushed aside while men scrounge through the furrows of life's fields, looking for scraps to satisfy their incessant hunger for meaning and fulfillment.

Life is so short for every man born. Only a small moment in the eternal ages to make a mark on his Creator's heart... What an opportunity man has been given to become one with his Creator in this miniscule moment of infinity!

Only the wise in heart redeem the time in these evil days. Only what is invested in the eternal has any meaning whatsoever.

I have wise friends in convents and monasteries. They have left the world to pursue the reality of eternity. They are called fools by the world, but they have been given a heavenly vision, a taste for God's holiness.

I leave My mark on seeking souls. My imprint of love makes them wholly Mine forever. How blessed they are to anticipate an eternity in My embrace and good graces!

Many will be ashamed on that day of reckoning. Their life will have been a sham of proud glory with no eternal benefit. Will you be wise, My friends? "Be Me all things consist."

Jesus,
Eternal Life

"Saints make every place a sacred spot to adore God."

June 29, 2016

"Souls throughout the centuries have been in pursuit of their Creator. Each soul was brought into this world to find its God. It is a journey of many hills and obstacles, each life on a unique path known to God alone. His will is performed beyond man's expectation or understanding.

God, in His splendor, can be known by His human creations. He has placed a spark in each heart, a light hidden in the soul. This light is the pathway into the heart of his Source, the Creator, his Father.

Men drown out the light. They pour water on it. They cover the light, because their deeds are evil. They will not come to the light for healing and direction. They choose to ignore the light, to pretend that it does not exist, this restless conscience within them.

Men know right from wrong before they are taught. This is the light of God in the heart, the gift of the knowledge of good and evil, which Adam tasted. Today, as in Adam's day, man disobeys Me consistently, turning away from My light to enter the darkness of the pride of life.

This light within your soul was created to diffuse from within. This light should grow until your entire body is filled with light. That is the transparency of holiness, letting My light find its way outside of you so that you can be that candle held aloft on a candlestick for all the world to see.

Do not stifle the light, My children. Look for Me within yourself and I will illumine your darkness.

As My light grows within you, you will shine forth as a beacon to the desperately dark souls on earth. You will give them hope. They will know that My kingdom is indeed within them, in the center of their being, just waiting to bathe them in My Essence of Light.

"I am the Light of Life." Come to Me to be lit up by My glory."

Jesus,
Light Bearer

June 30, 2016

"Your life is a journey into My Heart. There is no other road that will give you the happiness you seek. Life is an illusion to souls bereft of My presence. In their seeking for earthly gratification, they bypass eternal bounty.

My path to glory is simple, but obscure. In obedience to Me you stay on the path of virtue, making time for intimate colloquy with Me daily. In this hidden state, you adorn your soul with My life. Daily you grow in grace and in the knowledge of Me and My will for you.

The simplicity of spiritual growth is all consummated in the statement: "Not my will, but Thine be done." Handing your will over to Me daily will keep you on My royal path to eternal glory. All spirituality hinges on this eternal precept: Hand your will over to the Blessed Trinity and leave it in His keeping. Keep your eyes on His hands as He directs you daily according to His good pleasure.

There are no intricate details to learn, no special skills to cultivate to learn the higher secrets of spiritual growth. Only one thing is necessary – to do My will alone daily.

Place yourself in My hands every morning and wait for Me to direct you. Joyfully thank Me for My watchcare and provision for each moment of your existence. This is faith: following the unseen hand that guides you.

Only the little children enter the kingdom of heaven because they allow themselves to be taught, guided, and directed by the eternal Godhead.

"You are not your own; you are bought with a price." Let Me take charge of My purchased property.

Let go of yourself. Let Me take full responsibility for all that you are.

You can trust My guidance, for I love you <u>with</u> <u>all</u> <u>My</u> <u>heart</u>!"

Jesus,
Gentle Lover

July 1, 2016

"The heart of an apostle is linked to My Heart. We have the same desires – the conversion of the world to God's holiness. Time is God's opportunity to carve souls into saints. It is a gift given to men leading to eternal life.

Man has abused the gift of time since the Garden of Eden. He has used time to gather riches, enjoy pleasures, and seek happiness. He does not see time as a gift and a grace from God. Time is given to you to perfect your soul in holiness, to become pure like the angels, to overcome the tests and trials of life to prove yourself wise before God.

Men waste time on meaningless activities to entertain themselves, to indulge themselves, to forget about the realities of eternity. They go forth daily seeking amusements and ways to make the minutes fly by uselessly.

I created time as a device to save your soul for an eternity with Me, to be a faithful member of My family, to enjoy My presence forever. Your life goal is to use time to your advantage by investing in eternal realities.

The remedy for this slothfulness is prayer and self-examination. Come before Me in humility and thank Me for the gift of time. Ask Me how to use time wisely and I will explain the value of every moment seeking My face.

The time is short. Death waits for no one. No one can control their time of exit from this earth.

Become wise, My children. Stop. Look at your life. How have you spent the past years of your life? How do you want to spend your very few remaining years?

The wise in heart will heed these words. The foolish will continue to squander the precious gift of time, throwing it away in nonsense.

Be wise, My children. Be wise."

Jesus,
God's Son

July 7, 2015

"Off in the distance you hear the rumblings of a world that has forsaken God, the Creator. The earth is filled with confusion and woe and the light grows more and more dim over souls. The prophet's voices are growing faint and unintelligible.

The heart of man has become a hardened wall through which the light of God cannot penetrate or shine through. As in the days of Noah and the days of Sodom and Gomorrah, men's hearts were wickedly evil, so in this time of history, all the moral walls have crumbled, and men live hedonistically, like wild beasts. They are never satiated with their sin but seek ever new and evil ways to prolong their rebellion against the natural order created by God.

Men are roaming throughout the earth to pacify their every whim and desire. God is not in all their thoughts. Thoughts of pleasure, wealth, gain, self-seeking fame and fortune overwhelm all that they pursue. The children follow along blindly, seeking earth's treasures in the newest gadgets and devices.

What will become of this earth, moldy and filth-ridden in sin? What will turn the tide of evil that waits like the crest of a wave to overtake mankind?

The Son of Man, Jesus Christ, looks out from the doors of heaven. He awaits the signal from God to return to the earth to rescue the just souls and to repay the evil souls with the currency they have longed for. "Sin, when it is conceived, bringeth forth death."

Stay in the heart of God, My loyal followers, who live in a world permeated with foul ungodliness. Stay in your prayer closets, interceding unceasingly for the souls of men, especially the pure and innocent children who are being swept into the tidal wave.

I am coming soon, My flock. Be faithful and persevere unto the coming of your Lord in great glory."

Jesus,
Warrior for God

July 18, 2017

"Holiness reigns in a purified heart, a repentant heart open to heaven's words spoken in secret. A gaze directed toward heaven is rewarded with heavenly peace and glory.

Man runs from God's embracing love. The heavens cry tears of unending sorrow upon this land of desolation and despair. Creation revolts against the depravity and degradation man has taken upon himself. The children of God have set up their idols in their hearts, bowing down in worship to the gods of this evil age. Resistance to the Holy Spirit brings despair and hopelessness.

Man roams to and fro throughout the globe searching for phantom treasures. His heart is heavy, laden down with sinful lifestyles. Repentance is far from his mind. His peace is spurned as he believes the lies of this evil age.

My children shine as lights in the darkness. They are perfumed casks of holiness, shining light into the dark corners of the world. I woo the world through their docile, obedient trust. My faithful ones are a beautiful and fragrant aroma rising above the world's squalor.

My chosen ones, you delight My heart. I am the great Forgotten One, hidden from the minds of men to their detriment. I will shine through you if you will allow it, and I will bring My wayward children home to My heart if you will let Me shine My light through you.

It is not of your doing. The work is Mine. Just let yourself be inhabited by My Holy Spirit. Allow Him to form you into an "alter Christus," a soul with My heart of love.

My chosen ones … how I love you! You are so dear to My heart. We will be together forever.

The journey is almost over. Stay faithful until our meeting. You will be greatly rewarded for your persevering love."

Jesus,
Greatest Lover

July 31, 2015

"The fibers of My heart are outstretched and taut as I see the sinful deeds and the blasphemous lifestyles of men on earth. They live lower than the beasts of the field. Their consciences have been seared by their sinful and erroneous ideas.

It truly is like it was in the days of Noah and the days of Sodom and Gomorrah. Man's heart is wicked and evil toward the innocent, slaughtering babies in the womb.

A severe oppression has settled over the earth, a dark cloud of gloomy despair. As man has rejected My light, the darkness has descended upon him.

Few and far between are the souls with true faith, those "having not seen, yet believe." They are tiny pinpoints of hope on the globe of the world, begging for God's forgiveness and mercy. They have been shunned and quieted, yet their voices shout to heaven in their prayer closets.

My question is: When I return, will I find faith on the earth? Can souls resist the world's value system and swim against the tide valiantly? Only I can give My children the strength and endurance to match the wits of the Evil One.

The days are flying by, My children. Only one life you are given. Recognize what is eternal. Recognize what is nothingness.

You are made of dust and your body will return to dust. Capture the soul moments, those treasures from the spirit realm that build up your souls.

This is eternal life beginning for you – an eternity with God. Prepare yourselves for this great gift."

Jesus,

Love

August 7, 2016

"The world has turned its back on Me. The light is being extinguished. Men reject the true light because their deeds are evil. The light is smoldering in My elect ones. They are not keeping the home fires burning brightly. They are roaming the world, distracted by so much information, the globalization of world events.

The only force that will change this decaying world is the Holy Spirit. Souls filled with the Holy Spirit are the powerhouses that can restore power to this world. As electrical systems shut down when hit by lightning, so the lights in the world have been shut down. There are no working generators to restore the power. Only My Spirit can bring electricity back to the power lines.

Many of My children are trying to restore the power by natural means – by words, by activities, by allurements. This does not work. Only supernatural things will ignite My light in souls. Only souls filled with My Holy Spirit can change the atmosphere of the world.

The Holy Spirit cannot dwell in impurity. He flees the impure. The life must change. Repentance must precede a life change.

Humble yourselves before Me, O Christian souls. Repent. Turn away from evil. Destroy the idols in your life. Flee all impurity. Dedicate your time to Me. Make time for prayer. Worship Me instead of your freedom.

Wake up, souls. The darkness has formed over the land. I need light bearers to rekindle the light.

Where are you, holy souls of courage? The world needs you."

Jesus, Seeker of Souls Willing to Lose Their Lives in This World For the Kingdom of Heaven

August 9, 2017

"The simplicity of a moment by moment encounter with the Infinite One. I am the voice of eternity. There is no time with Me. I see yesterday as today and today as tomorrow in every present moment.

Learning to live in the present moment is a heavenly gift which very few souls attain in this life. They pine over the past or worry about the future. It is an endless cycle of wasting precious moments in the present.

"Now" is when you can touch God. "Now is the day of salvation." Now you can talk to Me. Now you can listen to My voice in your heart. Yesterday is over and gone. It is useless to you today. Ask Me for the gift to live in the present moment. Then your life becomes a beautiful fragrance of love ascending to My heart. Our souls touch and we live in the communion of the present moment.

Life will end one day and all that you will hold on to will be the precious moments of intimacy and friendship with your loving Father and Creator. The test of life is your love and friendship with your God who gave His Son for your redemption.

How do you love Me? You spend quality time with Me. You speak to Me. You listen to Me. You serve and obey My inspirations all given to you for your growth in holiness.

Your daily walk with Me is the most important aspect of your life. It must become your priority. You will desire nothing else on the day of your passage from this life.

Love Me as I love you. Listen to Me as I listen to you. This is a holy friendship that will last forever.

Take nothing for granted. Cultivate this great garden of delights. You will enjoy the fruits eternally."

Jesus,
Gardener of God

August 12, 2015

"The blood of Jesus cleanses us from all sin."

Who in these days speaks of My blood, which was used to purchase the souls of men, the price of man's redemption?

There is much talk in these days of pathways to the divine, but there is little talk of My redeeming blood that was shed for the sins of the world.

My shed blood was carried into the holy presence of God by angelic ministers. This blood is the efficacy for man's sinful condition. "Without shedding of blood, there is no remission for sin."

Mankind does not want to think or talk about alarming subjects such as blood and crucifixion. These troubling topics are off limits to the world's way of thinking. Man does not think as God thinks. He is limited in his thought processes and perceptions. It is an act of faith to believe in the power of the blood of Jesus.

My human blood was shed on earth as ransom for My kidnapped children. Sin had kidnapped them and had held them captive. I bought their release with My blood. It is through this blood that man has access to My Father.

"When I see the blood, I will pass over them..." The Israelites were saved from the angel of death by the blood of the lamb sprinkled on the lintels of their homes. Even today, when My Father sees My blood sprinkled on the hearts of My children, He grants them access to the heavenly kingdom.

In your prayers for souls, remember to speak of My blood to My Father. This blood is your passport to heaven. This blood will wash away your sins. This blood will heal your blindness and anoint your eyes with eyesalve so that you can see clearly.

My blood is powerful!"

Jesus, Blood Donor for the Human Race

August 18, 2017

"All of life is a continual surrender to grace. My grace is light that enters a soul that is open to receive it. My grace is an ocean of love that surrounds every repentant heart.

Grace is God's love manifesting His beauty to men of earth, men made of dust but raised up to the realm of God's supernatural existence.

My children of grace will reign with Me eternally in love and peace. What a happy future awaits you, My children of light! You will bask in My love eternally. You will live in My love forever!

You can enjoy the grace of My peace and love even now while living on earth. You can live moment by moment in My radiant light, reflecting My beauty to the world.

Let My light infuse you moment by moment by turning your heart to Me in prayer and contemplation. It is not hard. It is a beautiful thing to contemplate your Creator who loves you. He will assimilate you into Himself and you will change the world around you from darkness to light, from unrest to great peace. The atmosphere around you will be filled with My fragrance and souls will be enticed to seek the eternal.

Heaven is always peeking through the dense clouds to draw souls into its splendor. Those that raise their eyes to heaven will recognize heaven's overtures.

"Look to Me that ye may be radiant with joy." Let Me shine My light through your countenance.

My rays of love and light will attract the moths of earth and I will transform them into butterflies of great color and beauty.

"All things are possible with God." Let Me do the impossible through your smiling face."

Jesus,
Radiance of God

August 19, 2016

"The crucifixion has been forgotten. The supreme sacrifice of My blood shed for all the souls ever created is unknown to those created by a loving Father. "If I be lifted up, I will draw all men to Myself." My crucifixion is the only bridge to heaven, the only door to an eternity with God.

My beloved children have forgotten My sacrifice of love. They have devised many means to preach the Gospel message, but the power of the Gospel is derived from the message of My bloody cross, My human sacrifice, My condescension to die for the sins of the world.

My holy blood is the gift I have given to men to be reunited with My Father. My blood speaks to My Father, lovingly opening the paths to heaven. "Without shedding of blood there is no remission of sins."

Man's reasoning and intelligence have blinded him to the simplicity of the Gospel message, My crucifixion for the sins of the world.

The message of the cross is foolishness to those who are perishing. Jews and Greeks seek for signs and wonders. Today mankind seeks redemption apart from the blood of the crucifixion.

Your message should be: "Jesus died for you. That's how much He loves you."

O holy blood of Jesus, the God-Man, may we never despise your efficacious healing power. You take away the sins of the world. Have mercy on us. You take away the sins of the world, receive our prayer.

The blood of Jesus cleanses us from all sin."

Jesus,
Who Shed His Holy Blood for You

August 20, 2015

"My children sit with Me in the morning hours gleaning the words of wisdom inspired by My chosen souls throughout the centuries. This is your mission – these few hours in the morning, seeking My presence, reading the words of My saints, staying alone with Me in silence while the world rushes outside the window.

Each soul is called to a unique mission. You are My Abigails. You keep Me warm with your presence. Day by day you faithfully sit alone with Me, keeping Me company, speaking to Me the words of My beloved saints, using your moments in time to be My real friend.

You are not always asking for things. You sit with Me to learn from Me, and I teach you the wisdom of the ages in the innermost sanctuary of your soul.

My rain of grace descends upon your head in silent condensation, keeping you in humble solitude. I am healing your soul; I am revealing Myself to you; I am re-creating you in My image, all the while that you are feeling that you are contributing nothing to My kingdom.

What great feats did My mother do? She sat alone in the silent house, pondering My truths, seeking My presence, obeying My will in all things. Exterior works did not define My mother's spirituality. Everything happened in her interior. She walked and talked with her God at every moment of her life.

God hid her away from the eyes of men. In His jealous love, He kept her for Himself. No man was worthy of her, only the God-Man.

In the same way, throughout the centuries, I have My chosen souls that I keep for Myself. They are My Abigails who keep Me warm in the night. They have been chosen from among men to live in My intimacy, My bed of love.

They are My lovers, the apple of My eye, My sweetest chosen ones. Their humble love has captured My Heart and I choose to spend every moment in their embrace.

Could there be a better Lover than I?"

Love

August 25, 2016

"What can the world give Me? What can a soul give Me? All that is created is Mine. What do I desire from My created humans?

The only thing they can truly give Me is their freewill offering of an undivided heart, a loving heart that desires to live for My glory alone.

Humans are frail and weak, made of the dust of the earth. They have no power apart from My gift of life to them. I want them to recognize their dependence on Me, to know that I love them as Father, to understand My great love for them which brought Me to earth to suffer and die for love of them.

Why are My children so hard-hearted toward Me? Why do they resist My loving advances, My desire to draw them closely to Myself? They consistently put up hindrances between us, obstacles to block My Holy Spirit's action in their lives. How grievous to My tender Spirit!

I told My disciples to become like little children to inherit the kingdom of heaven. Children are innocent, pure, open, loving, and easily led. They trust implicitly. They freely rejoice in all circumstances. They love with a pure and fervent heart.

This is the love I seek from My chosen ones ... love from a pure and humble heart. I am not looking for heroic actions. I am looking for pure intentions, simple glances of trust, gentle entreaties and hearts open to hear My promptings.

O My little children, I will help you. Come to Me to be healed and reborn into a child of heaven. There all souls walk in the innocence and purity of children. There all souls rejoice in the freedom and liberty of being children of God.

I am here for you, My little ones. Come to Me. I await your arrival."

Jesus,
God's Arms of Love

August 26, 2015

"The world of the spirit is infinite and eternal. There is no end to its height and depth. Horizons broaden daily as you sit with Me exploring the endless possibilities of our life together. I am Infinity. Man is limited and narrow in all his thinking and daily activities. He has not discovered the All of life, a "life hidden with Christ in God," the highest and most profound abiding in the heart of God-Creator.

Look at My world. There is no end to the varieties of plants and animals and colors and circumstances. Life energy continuously swirls and grows as the planet rotates. The heavenly bodies faithfully stay in the orbit I have assigned to them to give light to the darkened earth. My creation is magnificent to behold, a rolling ball of blue suspended in space, kept in existence by My loving embrace.

Little ones, you have the joy of entering My kingdom world, a place beyond man's intelligence to grasp. Only the Holy Spirit can reveal who I am and what your future holds. It is a glorious eternity of realms beyond your imagination. All you need do to enter is to love Me. Such a small price to pay for eternal life in joyful bliss in My world!

Look to Me that the radiance of My kingdom may shine through your eyes. Let Me cast My ray of light upon your entire being so that My glory may shine on your earth."

God,
Glorious Spectacle of Eternal Light

August 27, 2017

"Quietness is fearful to many people. It is a lonely void that brings sadness and feelings of futility. It is empty and appears meaningless. Noise dulls self-interpretation and pondering. Man continues to run full force; restless, agitated, and driven. There is no peace. Silence gives peace.

Silence opens the door to the spiritual realm. It breaks through earthly barriers. It opens heaven. Very few souls heed the call to silent encounters with God. In the frenzy of life, they never encounter the silent meeting with their God and Creator.

Life could end at any moment in time. This should be taken into consideration by fragile man, yet it isn't thought about. Death stares man in the face daily, yet man sidesteps the eternal issue.

O man, on the day of your death, how will you think? Will you be joyful and prepared, or caught unawares? This is something you should deeply meditate through. Your last day will come. You will give an account of your days on earth. They are few, but very important.

You have been given the gift of life. Do not take this precious gift for granted. Understand that the gift of life on earth is hastening to an end. Each day brings you a day closer to eternity. Ponder well how you live."

Jesus,
Timepiece for Eternity

August 31, 2015

"The Spirit groans on earth in the hearts of My chosen ones. Rebellion and chaos rule in the hearts of men and the Spirit grieves over their blindness.

The Holy Spirit is the song of love ascending to the Father's throne. He is the perennial praise of the Father filtering through the clouds.

My Holy Spirit seeks an entrance into the hearts of men, but the way is blocked by sin. He cannot enter a darkened heart that clings tightly to sin. All must be surrendered to God before the Holy Spirit can truly inundate and captivate a soul. He beckons My chosen ones to take the high road, the highway of holiness. It is a road diametrically opposed to the ways of the world.

The highways of earth are filled with pleasure seekers, idolaters, and blasphemers. The heavenly highway is filled with souls on their knees imploring for the salvation of the world.

The Spirit blows where He wills, like the wind. He can be captured by an open heart. He seeks a pure dwelling place in which to reside. He constantly calls out to the sons of men, pleading them to repent and be converted. He is found in all the narrow byways of earth.

Call Him incessantly, My chosen few, for He seeks an entrance into the interior of your soul. He seeks to fashion you into another Christ on earth. He seeks to fill your heart with joy from heaven. He seeks to form you into the image of a holy son of God.

As your praises ascend, God's graces descend. The Holy Spirit, the perennial praise of the Father, will praise God through you. Allow Him the space He needs to glorify the Father in your life. Open every door within you to the light of His presence.

Your joy will be full as you become one."

Jesus,
Voice of God

September 18, 2016

"How willingly I share My words with you! To open hearts, I pour forth Myself.

God's goal in creating man was relationship. He wanted to bear children that would love Him eternally. His heart was drawn out to these lowly men made of dust, so weak and feeble. He created them in His image, desiring to walk with them in friendship. He handed man the power over His will, wanting man to love Him in return of his own accord.

Man became a rebellious son, turning away from his father's goodness to walk his own path. God's grieved heart, wounded with love, stepped back to allow man to make his perilous choice of evil over good. All heaven stood aghast at such complacency on God's part as He allowed man to rebel and run away from His goodness.

The angels were judged swiftly and harshly when they rebelled, but man was pursued with God's loving gaze, the gaze of a father grieving for his only son.

In God's wisdom, He sought man's freewill return to His heart. He sacrificed His own Son to provide an open door for man's return. He awaits anxiously on the threshold, welcoming all who return to His loving arms, His fatherly embrace. "All that come to Me, I will in no wise cast out," He proclaims so lovingly.

In My love for My Father, I came to earth to offer the perfect sacrifice of appeasement for the sinful rebellion against God's holiness.

I wanted My Father to smile again over His wayward children on earth. I wanted to restore the beautiful relationship that was destroyed by Adam's disobedience.

My heart was filled with My Father's love for His children. I became the open door to bring His children home again.

I love the children of God in the world. I long to embrace them all, but I am rejected. What a grief to My soul! What a grief to see My Father's love rejected!

Souls, understand My love for you. I gave all of Myself for you because I love you and I love My Father."

Jesus,
Your Elder Brother

September 22, 2016

"You are My friends. I have so few friends on earth. Many souls are acquaintances, many souls are, as it were, employed by Me, many souls speak My name, but few souls are My friends. Friends spend quality time together getting to know each other. How else can you get to know Me if you do not spend time alone with Me?

What is a friend? A friend listens, a friend empathizes, a friend understands, a friend gives of herself, a friend is loyal and true, a friend is available in time of need. My friends are interested in My plans, My guidance, My thoughts.

Acquaintances pass by in the night, but friends stick closer than a brother. To draw near to My heart is to become My friend. I can speak freely to a friend. I can guide and direct a friend without disturbance. I can count on a friend.

To be a friend of God is no small thing! It is an oasis in a desert land. It is refreshment in the arid seasons of life.

My friends, will you trust Me when trials burden your spirit? Will you stay by My side, docile to all I bring into your life? Will you bring joy to My heart as you joyfully surrender all of yourself to Me? Will you wait patiently for the leading of your gentle Friend in all things? Will you trust and not be afraid?

Friends walk together in harmonious agreement. Stay by My side in love as all things unfold in your life. You know that I have been faithful to our friendship, that I have never let you down.

My forever friends, how I love you! It hurts My heart to see you worry and fret. I know what I am doing in your regard.

Trust Me on this! I am working behind the scenes.

Trust, rest, and be full of joy, for you are truly My friends, My best friends."

Lovingly,
Jesus,
Your Friend for Life

September 29, 2016

"Life is a series of new beginnings. You fall, and you rise over and over again throughout your life. Your human nature constantly drags you down to the earth from which you were created.

Your spirit within you longs to soar into the heavens like the birds, flying above the earth with Jesus, yet you are held down by the slender cords of attachments.

Souls are held captive by many strings binding them to earth: strings of relationships, strings of possessions, strings of habits, strings of self-will. These strings need to be cut one by one in order for your spirit to soar to God.

Trials are the scissors that cut the strings. Each trial is carefully designed to cut a string holding you to earth. One by one these strings are cut throughout your life until the last string is cut. Then your soul can ascend to heaven to live with Me eternally in great joy.

I work unceasingly in your soul to carve My image in your features. I am not welcomed in the world for My ways are not the ways of the world. As the strings are cut, the disparity becomes very evident that you do not belong to this earthly land.

You were created for heaven. You are the one holding yourself to earth by your attachment to temporal things.

Release your grip on this world, on all you think you desire. Let Me cut the strings holding you to the earth.

Learn to live the life of heaven upon earth so that souls can follow you to My kingdom.

It is easier than you think. Let go and you will rise like a balloon into the spiritual spheres, the realm of eternity."

Jesus,
Hot Air Balloon Master

October 5, 2017

"Forward on to the goal, the prize of eternal life awaiting you in the heavenlies. Let nothing divert your course. It is a daily battle to stay on track, but you must be prepared to prioritize your daily activities.

Sit down and think about how you spend your waking hours. Are there hours wasted on nonessentials? You must cultivate the spiritual in every task if you are to grow in grace and in the knowledge of My life in you.

When you fall, and you will, rise and begin again. Fight the good fight of faith daily in all you encounter. Do not brood over your failures or fall into negative and despairing thinking. Stand up, face the day, look to Me for moment by moment direction, and I will arm you with My strength.

Put your daily will and effort into your relationship with Me. I am the daily 'Forgotten One' by My children. I wait for them to recognize My presence and willingness to help them.

I have told you: No time with Me is _ever_ wasted. You need this time of direction and solitude. You need to stop running the daily race of earthly distractions.

Time is running out for the world, and all these earthly possessions will fade into nothing. All that will remain standing will be your strengthened spirit confidently holding your place as a child of God.

So many have lost hope and strayed from the narrow path. They need a beacon in the night to point the way to Me.

You will feel solitary and alone as you stand giving forth My light, but even though you do not see the fruit of your endeavors to stand strong in Me, I am working valiantly in the backgrounds of life in men's souls.

"Having done all, to stand." Stand tall in My love and watchcare for you.

"I will never leave you or forsake you."

Jesus,
Guardian of Life's Paths

October 7, 2016

"The wind blows strongly outside your window. The wind, though silent, is speaking to the world. It is howling and raging because it is lamenting man's sinful condition.

Nature is not in harmony because man has rebelled against his Creator. The wind is calling out for men everywhere to repent of their evil ways and sinful lifestyles and to return to a holy way of life, the life the earth was created for.

Tragedy seems the only remedy to wake mankind up from his downward descent in life. The more freedom and pleasure they possess, the farther they stray from God.

In these tragic moments they rediscover the meaning of their existence. They see how frail and tenuous the cord of life really is for them. They look away from the temporal things that consume them toward what is real and lasting.

I do not like to punish My children. They punish themselves by defying the laws of nature. In their willfulness, they deny God Most Holy and nature cries for them in their shame.

Do not fear, My chosen ones. I have you safe in the palm of My hand. I will use you to illuminate those in the darkness.

Your life will shine brightly before them. They will see the folly of their ways and turn back to the ancient roads, the holy roads of God.

Trust in My care for you, children of My heart. My heart is grieved for My world of lost souls.

Help Me bring them back home into My heart."

God,
Forsaken Father

"I will make you a saint."

October 8, 2015

"The beauty of this moment of your life is My gift to you. To an attentive soul, I give all of Myself.

Heaven is a land of beauty and joy. The sparkle of eternal life with God colors everything. What is not My joy to bring heaven to earth to a soul open to My love!

I love to shower My attentive and chosen souls with beautiful gifts on earth. I am a loving Father wanting the best for My children.

Look up into the heavens. See the beauty of the sky, so ethereal and inviting. It is the covering over earth which separates the human from the divine.

Life is so much more than human beings can see. They are lost in their daydream lives, never living the present moment in all its glory. Breathing My pure air, admiring the beauty of nature, reveling in My gifts to you – this is the purity that can be achieved on earth.

Remember I told you that earth is the playground for My children? I watch to see how they play on My earth. Are they kind to their playmates or do they hoard the equipment and refuse to share with others? Are they bullies, or do they help the weak?

Do they proudly shut themselves off from others or do they come to the aid of the weak and defenseless? Do they love as I love? Do they appreciate My gifts? Do they appreciate Me?

I am the truly unselfish One. I share all I have with my souls on earth. I am not a cruel miser. I desire to inundate My children with gifts.

All I ask for is a thankful heart."

Jesus,
Gift Giver from the Real World

October 9, 2015

"Look at My beautiful earth – gifts from My kind hand. All on earth is gift from God. Does man realize what a gracious and beneficent and loving Father he has watching over him?

How I long to pour out countless blessings on mankind, yet they reject all My offerings! They choose to live life on their own terms without My interference.

What they do not understand is that My offer to them is abundant life, victorious daily living, joy beyond expression, confidence amid life's turmoil and an eternity of bliss – yet they reject all I have to offer. They turn away from Me in disgust. They are prodigals running away from the source of all they have ever been given.

I understand their frailty and ignorance. I wait for them just like the father and the prodigal son. I let them realize that life is futile without a connection to My divine life. I subtly introduce gifts and graces to prod them to remember Me.

I am so patient and compassionate toward them. They are unruly children, discovering the world for themselves. They seek to be free of a restraining parent.

Ultimately, life will disappoint them terribly. Tragedies, losses, sorrows, bad decisions – these hidden graces will make them stop to reconsider their direction in life. And there I will be waiting at the crossroad, hoping that they will choose My road of abundant life and love.

"I will forgive them and love them freely," for My mercy is exhaustive and compelling. I will welcome My errant children into My kingdom, wiping away their tears and soothing their regrets. The world thinks I am a mean God.

How they misunderstand My heart of love."

Your Loving Father
Who Communicates His Heart To You

October 9, 2016

"My heart is your heart. I care so much about all these trivialities in your life. So many details keep your mind occupied with the things of earth.

All is peace and joy in My kingdom. An eternity of peace and joy awaits you. Can you see your homeland in the distance? It is nearer than you think.

Life is so short. Time never halts for anyone. Soon you will face death as every soul created has faced that final door. You will look back on your life with a different eye. You will realize the uselessness of everything in the world. The life of the spirit will open up before you and the glory of holiness will appear in all its beauty.

Why don't you live now in the light of eternity? Why waste your time thinking of senseless things that will pass away? Sow to your spirit. Shun and despise the flesh for someday it will lie rotting in a grave.

Time alone with Me will give you a heavenly and eternal perspective. I will give you My eyes to see the reality of your life. The veils will be lifted, and you will see that life is a masquerade, that what you think is real is just a fantasy.

Rise above the earth and its vision. Ask Me to give you My eyes to see what is really happening. My vision is eternal. Your vision is earthly and limited.

Allow the Holy Spirit to invade your space of life. He will open your eyes to eternity. He will show you your homeland, waiting for you beyond the skies.

"Come away with Me, My beloved," He will whisper to you. Follow His voice as He leads you into the holy land of My Presence."

God,
Your Eternal Father

October 11, 2017

"The heavens are higher than the earth, yet they reside in your heart. You can live in heaven while dwelling on earth. I am heaven. As you abide in Me, you live in heaven's fragrance.

Everything on earth is pushing away the Creator of all that exists. If you seek Me within the secret depths of your heart, you will find Me.

Look to Me that you may be radiant with My light, for "I am the light of the world." My children of light are the candles in the world's darkness. Let Me shine My light through you.

So great is the love story between God and man! A condescending yet eternal love awakens the divine in man.

Heaven is as close as your next breath. Breathe forth My holy name and you will experience heaven. "I am all things to all men." All peace, all joy, all purity, all truth.

If you abide under My shade, you will exude My fragrant attributes to a world that has lost sight of the beauty of holiness. A holy life is the pearl of great price to a soul breathing his last breath on his deathbed. The greatest fear, death, can be faced with confidence by a soul that has loved Me.

I have gazed upon you as you have gazed upon Me. Time spent gazing upon Me transforms your soul. Love grows in these gazing moments. My peace descends into your heart and you then know that "all is well."

Let My gentle Mother lead you into My embrace. Her holiness is your example to follow. She leads souls to the Blessed Trinity."

Jesus,
Joyful Son of God

October 13, 2017

"I have called you to this place to comfort My heart. I am rejected of men. So few believe My story. So few trust My love. So few are obedient to My commands. Where is faith in this world given over to sinful pride?

"As it was in the days of Noah, so shall it be in the days of the coming of the Son of Man." I knew these days would come, but they are very painful to My loving and merciful heart.

I know that your life seems veiled in obscurity, but that is the way I deal with those I love. The obscurity of Joseph's life is a wonderful example of My higher purposes for a soul being ordained for the greater good of the world.

There is no sidestepping the royal road of the cross, following in the footsteps of Christ crucified. The cross is your banner of true life, leading you to holiness and purity.

Suffering purifies all intentions. Life is not about prosperity and happiness, popularity and success. True life is walking the hidden and obscure path of the holy cross, suffering, and affliction.

Why are you amazed when you are rejected, scorned, and misunderstood by those you've held in your heart in love? My life was constant rejection and terrible treatment by those I was laying My life down for.

You ask Me to transform you into an "alter Christus," yet you balk when the process begins. If you desire to follow My footsteps, you must accept all that happens in your life as My ordained will for you. As Shimei threw stones at David, the anointed king, David proclaimed: "It is the Lord's will. Let him throw the stones."

You will constantly encounter the opposition of the world if you intently follow Me, yet I desire that you stay on the royal highway of the redeemed, fellowshipping with Me for courage and strength.

Do not look for answers or comfort from people on earth. They cannot help you as I can. They cannot feed the inquiries and desires of your soul. They have no answers to give you.

I challenge you to run to Me when you are opposed, rejected, or hurt. I will comfort you. I will give you wisdom to respond as befitting a holy life.

Do not be discouraged. You are pressing forward in faith. You have not turned back in the day of battle.

You are seeking the highest calling – life under the shade of the Almighty God. How He adores you!

He is LOVE!"

Jesus,
Your Brother

October 16, 2017

"Joy arises in the heart of a soul dedicated to God's will. He skims over the earth's surface, barely touching the soiled ground, his conversation in heaven.

It is a blessed life to be God's friend on earth. God seeks loving friends, those that appreciate and discover His love.

To converse with God in your heart is to live a life of heaven on earth. God's presence brings peace, joy, and sweet love to the heart. A new realm of sweetness enlightens everything. The dark veil on earth is lifted. Eyes are lifted to the heavens, imploring grace for fellow earth travelers.

God calls whom He wills into intimate fellowship with His Trinitarian life. "Many are called, but few are chosen."

A life lived in God's intimate embrace is truly the greatest gift ever given. What a thought – Heaven is looking upon you with great love!

A soul in love with God desires to do all things with meticulous care and gratitude. A soul in love with God does not want to waste one moment on nonessentials. A soul in love with God has one goal – to please God in all things.

My loving favored souls live humbly on earth, unnoticed by men, but well known in heaven. They go forward in hope, glorifying their Love by a holy life.

These souls beg constantly for more grace to love as God loves. He answers these fervent prayers lavishly. He is kind and merciful.

To have eyes for God alone is the greatest gift sent from another realm, the realm of LIGHT."

Jesus,
Light Dweller

October 20, 2015

"You are progressing and learning about My will every day. You fall a lot, you question your path, you doubt your ascent, yet you press on, much to My delight. "Rome was not captured in a day," they say, and holiness also is a continual process of rising and falling as each occasion arises. Unless I bless you with the gift of instant holiness of heart, you must insistently and persistently stay on the path set before you, not allowing yourself to be discouraged, but pressing on.

You can make the path easier by relying more on My help than on your own stratagems. You can silence your chatter, inwardly and outwardly. Only in peace can you hear My directions clearly. Continual thinking and talking drown out My holy inspirations. In peaceful quietness, walk softly on the earth. Allow My Holy Spirit to gently lead you in every situation. Turn to Him with all your decisions. He will point out My way of doing things. My way is the holy way.

I want you to live in peace for the remainder of your life on earth. You have lived in chaos for too long. I long to truly be your Shepherd that leads you on paths of righteousness beside the still waters of peace. Follow Me as a docile little lamb follows the Shepherd's lead. Let Me take care of everything. Drop all control and let Me control your life. The result will be a beautiful and peaceful life with Me.

How I love you, My children!"

Jesus, Shepherd of the Lowly Lambs

October 10, 2015

Jesus, what do you want me to do today?

"I want you to live in peace.

Savor every moment of this short life.

Do your duties faithfully and with great love, as unto Me.

Love every soul you meet today.

Pray for every soul you see today.

Tell Me you love Me throughout the day. How I love to hear your words of love!

Be docile to the Holy Spirit's inspirations within your soul today. Let Him lead you.

Meditate and pray the Rosary with love and respect for My gracious mother.

Do not worry but pray. Accept all things that happen in gracious peacefulness of soul."

October 18, 2017

"The prayers of a pure soul spring into heaven with the speed of lightning.

Purity opens the doors of heaven speedily. These prayers are brought into God's throne room borne on the wings of the mightiest angels.

Few souls have known the power of prayer. "The effectual fervent prayer of a righteous man availeth much."

Purity of heart is a great gift from God's pure heart. He bestows this gift upon the meek and humble, those that know their nothingness.

God's favor rests so gently upon a pure heart. A pure heart is a heart that has been cleansed of selfish pride and willful passions.

A pure heart is of great beauty. It shines out above the ugliness of the world's power systems.

"The heart of man is desperately wicked, who can know it?" Man, in his pride, has abandoned his Creator. In his insolence, he has chided God. He has lost sight of spiritual childhood. He is a god in his own eyes.

My eyes are on the pure souls on earth. I protect them as the apple of My eye. I hold them very close to My heart. They are My dear ones on earth, those that have "made a covenant by sacrifice."

My littlest children gather around My table, the altar where My Son resides on earth. They taste of

My goodness in Holy Communion. They eat My fruits of goodness and mercy. These are My littlest souls, those that have made themselves children in My sight, trusting Me, depending on Me, sincerely and eagerly following Me.

"They shall walk with Me in white, for they are worthy."

Jesus,
God's Lamb

October 20, 2017

"I am the Light of the world. He that followeth Me shall not walk in darkness." My truth shall illumine your footsteps. As a child walks hand in hand with her father, I shall hold your hand into eternity and beyond.

"Look to Him that your face may be radiant with joy."

"The joy of the Lord is your strength."

"In Thy presence is fullness of joy."

My light brings great joy to your countenance. Souls can feel the peace in your smile when you are animated by Me.

I desire to walk the streets in your person. If you will allow it, My powerful presence will shine forth as in the days of My life on earth. Surrender yourself completely into My embrace. I will do the rest.

I seek surrendered souls to do My greatest works. My power is gentle and draws souls to goodness and truth. I will penetrate your being with My presence.

You will feel like an onlooker as great spectacles of conversions occur. You are just the channel of My grace. Always remember your nothingness. All grace and power are My gift to you to draw others to Myself and to glorify My holiness in the world.

Turn to Me always, asking: "What is Your will, my God? Live Your will in me at this moment" and I will walk the earth in your body. No place is left unchanged where I have trod.

Do not despise the days of little occurrences, seemingly insignificant in human terms. I do My greatest works in secret among the lowly.

Have faith in My promises to you. "God's will be done" is your motto, your life work."

Your Father of Love

October 22, 2015

"Each day unfolds in a spectacle of glory awaiting the deeds of man. How will a man live this day? Will he recognize the Creator of all that exists and revel in His beautiful creation or will he live in his own world of unreality to what is important in life?

Each soul has a unique path of holiness to become what God has created him to be. How few souls realize this godly potential! They get caught up in earth's schemes and forget their reason for existence. They have eyes, but they do not see; ears, but they do not hear.

What do I require of you? I ask you to walk humbly with Me all the days of your life. Let Me show you My purpose for creating you. Let Me keep you on the unique path I have chosen for you. Let Me speak to you as I spoke to Adam and Eve in the Garden of Eden, friend to friend.

You make things complicated, men of earth. I know you are made of dust. I know you are very weak. I know how susceptible you are to falling away and getting distracted from your true purpose.

I am not asking for heroism beyond your strength. I am asking you to be an obedient child, holding your Father's hand all the days of your life. Be gentle and docile, easily led by My Holy Spirit.

Do not make things complicated. Do not think much – love much, as a child loves spontaneously.

In quietness, solitude, and moments lingering in My presence, you will come to understand what I desire from you. I have come to set you free from your worries, fears, and concerns. Rely on Me for everything. I long to be everything to you.

I am here with you though you do not feel My physical presence. That is faith – knowing I am with you without visible evidence. "The just shall live by faith." How this pleases Me!

Allow Me to live in you today. What a beautiful day we will share together!"

Jesus,
Lover of Souls

October 25, 2016

"It takes but a moment to look into My eyes in the midst of your daily activities. You do so much on your own when I am so willing to help you, to be involved in your projects, to give My blessing to your works.

Do not let the hasty happenings of your day drag you away from My presence. I am always with you, directing your steps silently.

As you acknowledge My presence, we work together, and the effort becomes joyful for you rather than confusing and harried.

It takes but a moment to ask for My guidance and opinion. I want to be a part of your day. I desire the intimate friendship of two lives intertwining throughout each occurrence.

I am here for you. Utilize My nearness and My help. I am here to bear your burdens. You take too much upon yourself and the burdens are too heavy for you. Let Me help you.

Slow down today. Enjoy the moments I've given you. Trust that all will be taken care of by My capable hands.

I miss our times of silence together. Your busy activity is keeping you from savoring "the best part," My holy presence within you.

All is as it should be. This trial was needed to show you what you are without My strength. I want you to rely on Me for everything! That is true union with your Friend and Creator.

All is well, My children. Take a rest today by basking in My holy will for you each moment.

Sing joyful songs in My presence. Singing is loving trust in action."

Your Father Who Loves You Infinitely

October 27, 2015

"Time is a gift. You can give this gift away to anyone anywhere. It has been given to you in order to prepare your soul for heaven. Who or what have you given My gift of time? Who has received your time, My gift to you to use profitably?

Does the television receive your time? Do the necessities of your body take up your time? Do people steal your time unprofitably? Books? Sporting events? Hobbies? Exercise? Social gatherings? Internet surfing?

I have given you the gift of time to use wisely for eternal profit. My gift of time is wasted and thrown away in many lives.

Addictions, pleasures, selfish pursuits, and vainglorious accomplishments have stolen many hearts. In return, souls hand over their time with no regard for the great gift they are discarding as garbage.

Only so many moments are allotted to a life. Once they are used up, all is over. There is no reclaiming lost time.

Every moment in time can be impregnated with My holiness. One glance in My direction will direct all your efforts to the best use of your time share.

Lives come and go. Fame, fortune, prosperity, popularity, experiences, strengths – at the moment of death, nothing matters but man's relationship with his Creator. Was it nurtured? Was it even considered?

My gifts are not used. How this grieves My heart, this heart that loves to give and receive back with interest!

Children, make friends with your greatest friend on earth – time. Let her teach you how to spend her wisely. She has only so many grains of sand to give you. Treasure each one!"

Jesus,
Time Giver

November 13, 2017

"The journey to eternal life in heaven is not easy. It is a daily battle against the flesh that always seeks the easy way out. In order to subdue the flesh, you must spend your days aware of My presence within you.

I am here to help you, to instruct you, to lead and guide you, but you must ask for My help. Continue to discipline your day around My presence within you.

It is a lonely and dying road in this worldly age, but the narrow road still beckons souls to trek to sainthood apart from the world. "Narrow is the road to life and few there be that find it."

Do not think that holiness requires no effort on your part. You must decisively turn away from the world to seek My face. This is no easy task when the fleshly appetites are the lot of every soul on earth. It is a warfare between spirit and flesh. You must choose.

Love opens the door to the path. The more your love is kindled, the less the world appeals to you. You then seek the higher life, the royal road, the highway to heaven where the saints and angels live. They long to help you on your journey. Ask for their prayers and assistance.

How many days do you have left on earth? You do not know. Time is extremely short, and eternity is forever. If only man would fathom this life-changing truth!

Live for heaven! Forget the earth – it is temporary. Strive manfully for the prize of an eternal reward.

You will then stand before Me unashamed at the judgment seat on that final day of your life on earth. You will be welcomed heartily, and your soul shall rejoice.

Keep the faith. Keep a heavenly perspective.

Keep asking. Keep seeking. Keep knocking."

Jesus,
Your Gentle Friend

October 26, 2015

"Are you ready to let go of all that you think that you are to let Me come into your life in My way? So many souls seek Me according to their plans. They have preconceived ideas about how I will intervene in all that happens to them. They play out their own little drama and attribute it to My workings. Man is afraid to let go, to relax into My arms in trustful rest. I wait for souls to get to the place of abandonment before I can freely work in them unhindered.

How could a potter shape a vessel unless it was without motion? Even so, My children come to Me for help but when I respond, they jump out of My hands to try to figure things out in their own way. I am not left free to help them … and so I wait for the opportune moment of complete and total abandonment to My will.

Abandon yourselves completely to Me, My children, and allow Me to help you. Let go of all your preconceived ideas and agendas. Allow Me to show you a new way to expand your limited horizons. You cannot do it on your own, children. You need My help and I am so willing to help you.

Become the dependent child I desire you to be. Let Me help you. Calm down; stop your running; sit quietly, listening for My words of instruction.

I know the answer to every question and every problem you have. Let Me help you through life. I am <u>so</u> willing!"

Love, Jesus,
Your Helper in Life

November 14, 2017

"As you journey to your homeland, the way becomes more narrow. I expect more from you, so the lessons become more individualized.

Everything has a purpose and a plan to sanctify you. You must see events with My eternal vision.

Trials and adversity will surely not be wanting, but what I want you to learn is how to handle them. Instead of taking everything at face value, you must see the bigger picture. To do that, you must immediately consult with Me on everything that confronts you. This is a beautiful way to live amid the daily confrontations. You must turn to Me in your heart and say, "Jesus, what should I do? How should I respond? What are you trying to teach me?"

This will be a new habit for you because your first response has been to speak immediately before thinking things through. You <u>must</u> learn to control your tongue to grow in sanctity.

The tongue is an unruly member that can drive you to ruin and completely destroy your peace."

November 28, 2016

"Letters from heaven come gently on the wind of a stilled mind, a quiet heart, a weaned soul. Heaven is always speaking to souls, but so few listen.

The quiet will feed your soul. Rushing dissipates all the treasures in the soul.

Nature praises God in quietness.

A holy soul seeks peace and quiet. Come away from the world's noise to the peace of your God. Let Him speak to your heart. He desires to rest in your soul.

God is a beautifully quiet Creator. He dwells in eternal silence and unity. Confusion and disarray are alien to Him. He seeks a peaceful, stilled heart to abide in gently.

"Be <u>still</u> and know that I am God."

Holy Spirit,
Whisperer

November 19, 2017

"In the silence you will hear My voice, but you must practice self-discipline to hear My voice in the silence.

The world calls you in every direction, but you must solemnly and soberly turn away from the world to seek the invisible and the eternal.

It is no easy task to keep oneself unspotted from the world. A pure soul is rare to find. Much renouncement is required. Abandoning yourself in all things to My good pleasure is difficult in a world full of distractions and obstacles.

Grace will be given to you if you ask in faith. Every time you pray, I give you a part of Myself. I am the answer to every prayer. I am all that exists. I have created all that exists.

The silence will teach you many things. It will answer all your questions. Find Me in the silence. I wait for you there. I will teach you My language of eternal silence, the rest and peace of God.

If you contemplate the silence of outer space, you will realize that God's immensity abides in the silence of infinity and beyond. Leave the earth's atmosphere. Join Me in the heavenly realms of the silent regions of God's stillness. We will not use words to communicate. We will think as one."

Jesus,
God's Silent Word

November 20, 2015

"Spiritual strides quicken in response to love. The more you love, the quicker will you grow in holiness.

Works are priceless, theology is a basic need, spiritual aspirations and desires are fruitful, yet without love, the fire has no wood to kindle.

Give me a soul with love in the heart and I will show you a true saint. Maybe this soul cannot read or write. Maybe this soul has no doctrinal aptitude. Maybe this soul is unlearned and unchurched. If there is love, there is God.

All souls have not been given the graces of doctrinal teaching. Maybe they have never picked up a spiritual book. How can they attain to sanctity? By love alone. God is love and he that abides in love abides in God.

"By their fruits you shall know them." "The fruit of the Spirit is love" foremost. A man may be learned in every area of spiritual formation, but if God's loving fruitfulness is lacking in his life, all that learning is straw to be burned.

I see that African woman living in a mud hut. She has never picked up a book or listened to spiritual teaching, yet her heart is on fire with love for her Creator. She is a saint.

Many learned men have a head full of knowledge, yet they have not truly met the Giver of this knowledge, the

God of burning love. They have good intentions, but they have mistaken the firewood for the fire.

The souls that are in love with Me radiate My atmosphere of loving peace. They do not judge; they love. They let Me do the judging. Their eyes are so blinded by love that it is nearly impossible for them to judge another. They love people into doing right.

Souls respond to this unconditional love. They follow this atmosphere of love straight into My Father's arms. Every soul craves love and when they find it, they run eagerly to embrace it.

Permeate your atmosphere with My love. My radiance through you will draw souls to My Father's Heart of love."

Jesus,
Greatest Lover

November 23, 2016

"A quiet, simple life is sought among My children of light. They shun the world's ways. They seek the peace of heaven. They cannot find it in the world's ways.

God is beautiful and quiet. He rests in peaceful, quiet, and contented souls. He does not shine forth in agitated lifestyles. He glows in the faces of His little children of light, those weaned from the world's ways.

In your hiddenness is your spiritual strength. You are renewed in the silent moments alone in My presence. Heaven comes to earth in your heart and it shows in your countenance. My light glows within a pure heart.

Let the world go, My daughter. Attend to My heart. Let the remaining years of your short life be spent in listening to My voice. Write down what I tell you so that others may hear My truths.

The world is hungry for Me, yet they cannot find Me. I desire to reveal Myself to them, but they cannot find the way. You must show them by your life of peaceful solitude. They must see the Christ looking at them from your eyes. Your peacefulness must radiate My light to them.

Words are not needed to display My brightness to the world. A pure heart, a loving desire for Me, a willingness to be led and guided along life's roads – these all attest to My presence within you.

I have been with you through these days of distress. I have led you through the hills and valleys. Everything in your life has a purpose. Accept all as My gift of love to you.

A new day has dawned. Let's walk the earth together today, you and I hand in hand. We will bless My children as we encounter each soul destined to meet us today.

You are Mine and I am yours. We are one."

Jesus,
Your Best Friend

November 24, 2017

"Roses are scattered around you every time you pray.

Flowers are a symbol of God's beauty and presence. They exist for His glory alone.

The Blessed Virgin Mary is likened to a beautiful rose, often called the Mystical Rose. Roses are a tribute to her great beauty of character and holiness of heart.

The human race was created pure in God's sight. Sin entered, and man's beauty was corrupted. Nature was cursed. Animals were subjected to man's inattentive cruelty. As in a fairy tale, darkness descended upon the earth until the Sun of Righteousness appeared to dispel and destroy the darkness of corruption and death.

Man's beauty was restored by the grace of the cross. The heart once veiled from God's holiness was opened by the light of the Anointed Christ. He "took captivity captive" and released man from the bondage of sin and corruption. God wiped man's heart clean and restored the broken fellowship. God's Spirit entered the soul of man again, making right what had been effaced by sin.

The door to holiness has been opened for you, men of earth. You must open your heart to receive this gift from God's kindness. He longs to restore you to the beauty He originally created you to be.

As you open your life to My work within you, I will reestablish you as a holy child of God, pure and beautiful in My sight. The refashioning will be painful and difficult, but all growth means change. Do not be discouraged at your slow pace. God is patient in His dealings with you. You are led like a child into His presence.

These moments alone in My presence stamp My holy imprint upon your soul. No time with Me is ever wasted. I am changing you. I am making you into the holy soul I created you to be.

Live in My loving embrace. I created you to love Me.

"Be still and know that I am God." You will hear My voice if you listen for it. I speak very quietly."

God,
Your Loving Father

November 25, 2016

"Do souls realize how short life is? Do they ever stop to consider their destiny? Souls are running madly on the world's course of action, rarely stopping to consider where they are headed unless, of course, they get sick or encounter a tragedy. Sorrows and tragedies can become gifts from heaven to stop souls from thinking that this short life is all there is to live for.

The earth has its own schedule and souls step in line to keep up with it. How rare is the soul that refuses to join the ranks of the followers being led in useless endeavors! The faster the rushing, the more chained you are to earth.

What can this earth offer you? Only temporal things that become dust in time. Tell Me what on this earth is eternal besides man's soul? Nothing. All fades.

The body ages and dies, the plants grow and die, the buildings crumble with age, popularity and fame make their exit at death. All become memories, only memories. And then the mind filled with memories dies. What then is left? The soul. So how should you live your short life? You should value only the things that benefit the soul.

The soul is eternal. It will never die. The soul can be beautiful or ugly, loving or hateful, hopeful or bitter. The goal of this short life is to make your soul beautifully pure, transparent, and radiant with God's face. The brightness of God's countenance should shine on your personage. His love and kindness should dictate all your actions.

This soul beautifying work should consume all your days.

Leave all else by the wayside. Think of your soul. Feed your soul. Pamper your soul by spending soul time alone with your soul Creator. He will beautify you with His radiant charm.

Wisdom has spoken."

The Holy Spirit, Soul Maker

November 29, 2016

"Time seeking heaven's help is imperative in your daily living. "Ye have not because ye ask not." Ask Me for what you need. Even though I know all your needs, I have made it clear that you are to ask to receive. That is the only mandate you need to receive My help.

Ask Me about everything! That is how we will walk together along the path of life daily. I will advise and counsel you. I will teach you My ways of living in this world that has basically rejected Me. You have to navigate expertly to remain on course among so many obstacles.

The world carries on day by day, but how many souls look to heaven for guidance? That is why so many lives are shipwrecked and blown off course.

I desire to guide you through peaceful waters, fluid channels so that your boat doesn't get stuck. With Me at the helm all will end well. We will take our boat ride to the gates of heaven and there I will drop you off into My Father's lap of love.

Be a docile child in our boat today. Let Me lead and guide you in all your decisions. You cannot steer your boat as beautifully as I can. I am the great Navigator, channeling My people through the waves of life's billows, steering them into heaven's ports. I am with you today in all you do. Please don't forget Me. Let Me help you."

Jesus, Helper

December 5, 2016

"The Holy Spirit speaks another language on earth. His voice transcends words. He speaks soul to soul. He is the hidden One of the Holy Trinity.

He brings no attention to Himself, but He is always working. His ways are not the ways of men. Man aspires to climb higher. He descends, like water, to the lowest place.

He seeks pure dwelling places for He cannot abide with sin. His holiness prevents any immersion into sin's domain.

The Holy Spirit is subtle, yet transparent. He is noiseless, yet powerful. He is hidden, yet prominent in all that exists. He flees from arrogance but runs quickly to the lowly.

Call upon Him. He will come to you. Let Him show you how to live your remaining days on earth."

Jesus,
Holy Spirit's Love

December 1, 2017

"These moments of direct contact and silence mold you into My image and likeness.

Your thoughts are in heaven. You realize how short and trifling life is in the light of eternity. Your heart beats as My heart, desirous of the Father's will in all things. This is truly heaven on earth, loving the Father's will and desiring to glorify Him in everything under the sun.

There is no better way to live than in intimacy with God Himself, your loving Creator and Father. He seeks sons and daughters to live lovingly in His infinite embrace. He seeks those willing to lose their short earthly life to be prepared for eternal life in His company.

God's majestic work is unfolding in the heavens. His magnificent designs from eternity past unfold before the eyes of the inhabitants that abide with Him eternally in the heavens. The angels desire to see the manifestation of the sons of God, those destined to reign eternally with Him.

The race is set before you, sons of men. It is the royal road of the cross, the opportunity to lose your life in this world to save it for eternal glory. Many have fallen by the wayside. Many have completely dropped out of the race in disappointment. Those that faithfully persevere in this dark world of sin will be greatly rewarded.

Walk on through the obscurity of a wicked earth, ever leaning to sin and sensuality. Pass by the dens of iniquity. Ignore the hollow laughter, for it will end with the season.

Look up to your God who beckons you to His home awaiting you in the sky.

All soldiers will be rewarded for their valiant valor in duty. They will be recognized in the heavenly courts on that day of reckoning when God will divide the sheep from the goats.

They will be My crown jewels, My beloved children of light, sparkling through the endless and glorious ages of eternity."

God of Hosts

*"My grace will make you
beautifully holy."*

December 7, 2017

"To walk forward unafraid in the darkness is a sign of great trust. My littlest ones walk forward in the darkness and confusion of life's turmoil despite the way all looks around them. They are unafraid. They trust Me.

Do you not believe that "all things work together for good to those that love God?" Why do you not trust all that I bring into your life as My means of sanctifying your soul to get you ready for heaven? Does freedom, rest, and getting your own way really matter in the scheme of things when you are in a battle to win heaven?

Souls battling are struggling, falling, and weary. They are not resting on couches of ease, enjoying peaceful, fun-filled days.

Life is a battle to become holy in a sinful world. Pure religion is to remain "unspotted by the world." My children are getting mixed in with the world's way of doing things.

The world does not walk God's path. The world has an entirely different roadway. I must not find My children on the wrong road on the day of eternal decision. There will be many regrets and much shame.

Narrow is the way that leads to heaven and "few there be that find it." It is lonely and dark the nearer you arrive at the gates of pearl. That is the royal road of the cross, following in the footsteps of your suffering Savior.

Keep your face looking at My face. Do not get distracted on your journey. I go before you. There is nothing to fear. Trust that I am leading you through the Valley of Death into My glorious eternal Kingdom of Light."

Jesus,
Your Love

December 9, 2017

"In the stillness and silence, you will hear Me speaking to you. It is hard for Me to shout above the noise of life. If you seek the pearl of great price, you <u>must</u> find the silence. Silence is hidden around every corner, but so few find it.

Silence is golden, as you have heard. Why? Because it is a treasure beyond the price of gold.

Heaven speaks to the silence. The realm beyond your time frame only manifests itself when your world ceases, the world of flesh and blood, to the world of spirit.

"Deep calleth unto deep..." Only the deep realm of the Spirit can reveal the hidden messages of God Most Holy. God is to be reverenced, and the heavenly court appear before Him in a profound silence. They are hushed in His presence.

Man does not understand reverence in worship. Man carelessly enters God's presence full of sin and noise. What an offense to a holy Creator beyond all imaginings!

God's holy children are obedient, silent, humble, and they know their place in God's kingdom. The first shall be last and the last shall be first. They seek the lowest place in humility before God's presence.

Mary, My exalted daughter, called herself the slave of the Lord. She understood God's magnificence and grandeur.

God is love, beauty, grace, and excellence; He is all-wise, tender, bountiful and meek Himself. He condescends to the lowest created thing in love and tenderness.

God loves all He has created. He longs to draw all souls into the splendor of His glory.

Children, forget what you think you know. Come, bowing low, in silence before God, your Father. He will embrace you in a hug you have never experienced.

He longs for you to love Him as He loves you. What a wonderful God!"

Jesus,
God's Beloved Son

December 16, 2015

"My heart is alive and beating in this world that has forgotten Me. The pulsating rhythms of the earth are the beating of My Heart, crying over man in his weakness. He has forsaken mercy and has chosen a tortuous path of self-indulgence and egocentricity over Love's calls and pleadings.

My heart has truly been broken by mankind's rejection. Who understands this heart of Mine, so tender and pure, so gentle and forgiving?

I am the Forgotten One, the forgotten Creator of all that exists. I created man for a loving relationship, but he has run away from Me and he has rejected My overtures.

Yet I cry out, I continuously plead with him, begging him to return to My loving Heart. He has run into the forest of jackals and demons, allured by the glittering sights and sounds of worldly enticements. He is led further and further into the dense forest. He cannot find his way out of the dense darkness.

My light bearers travel deep into the forest holding candles of hope high, leading the way out of the darkness, but they are shunned and ridiculed, made fun of and mocked. Their gentle hearts unite with My sorrow for mankind.

My saints crisscross each other through the darkness, holding their lamps high as they greet each other in

Love's relief. They are the soldiers of light piercing the dark forests of sin, rescuing the perishing.

The forest is ready to be folded up, nearing the completion of the ages. Those that have chosen the dark abyss will remain within its confines. "Those that turn many to righteousness shall shine as the stars forever and ever."

The light of heaven is dawning, My people. Be faithful to the course I have placed before you. Keep your focus on the eternal, the home I have prepared for you, as I await you in glory.

Time is short. "Redeem the time, for the days are evil ..."

Jesus,
God's Warning to Wandering Souls

December 18, 2017

"Communication with heaven is real. You can pass over into the realm of spirit any time you take your eyes off the sense world and silently search into your heart for My pleasure.

"Behold, I stand at the door (of your heart) and knock." I am <u>always</u> available to you. How can you fellowship with Me? By entering the door of stillness and silence; by seeking My peaceful Presence within you.

As we meet together in this quiet place, we can converse around the dining table; we can sit restfully on the sofa; we can walk hand in hand; we can recline together in restful accord. You can converse with Me about anything. I will be your best friend with the wisdom of God to answer every one of your questions or address all your fears with My guidance.

Why do I knock in vain perpetually in some souls? They are off running in the world, mesmerized and attracted by temporal castles of apparent beauty and fulfillment. I cannot get their attention. They are not living the abundant life that has been offered to them by My Father.

Heaven speaks. So few are listening. My friends hear My slightest whisper. They wait upon Me in the silent hours. We commune beautifully, and I rejoice in them.

They are My jewels which I keep in special coffers, My love and friendship coffers in heaven. They are gentle and trusting like My sweet Mother. They love Me with a mother's self-sacrificing love.

The beauty of a soul in love with God surrounds their human frame like a halo of grace and majesty. In their hiddenness, their beauty glorifies God. They are members of My holy family in heaven.

The days are coming when you shall see the King in His glory and majesty. He shall grasp your hand in friendship and you will exult in your heart that God opened your heart to His holy friendship."

Jesus,
Friend of God's Children

December 20, 2016

"My thoughts toward you are peace. I am Peace.

It is stated: "Peace is the tranquility of order." I am Order. I am Tranquility.

"I am all things to all men." "By Me all things consist." All that your eyes look upon show you My Essence.

There is no striving in My world. Man strives from the moment of his birth. My peace ends all striving. My tranquil peace rests in love.

I live and reign in a soul of quiet peace. How do you acquire My restful peace? By abiding tranquilly in Me moment by moment. By letting Me lead and guide all that you do. By trusting My omnipotent designs over your life.

My peace abides among the lowly and humble of heart who have quieted their ambitions. They gently wait for My direction in every encounter. They do not rush ahead of My will for them. They truly are weaned children. They have learned to sit alone quietly with Me, waiting for My word to touch their hearts.

The greatest saints have been the most peaceful souls. They have found their identity in Me. They do not need to 'find' themselves. They have found Me, their Source.

They are set apart from the world of sense to cultivate the spiritual realm. They have died to earth's allures and glamorous offerings.

The body means nothing to them in this world of body idolatry. They worship the Creator over the creature.

These are My saints living in the world today, the apple of My eye."

Jesus,
Saint Lover

December 19, 2017

"Heaven's splendors are reenacted at every Mass.

The supreme sacrifice of Jesus Christ is gloriously remembered in heaven, the sacrifice of all sacrifices for the redemption of the human race. The angels gather in festal gathering, bowing their heads in a holy hushed reverence, contemplating the condescension of God made man.

God abides among His reverential friends, those that contemplate His holiness. God gives man the gift of time to become friends with his Creator. So few humans receive this gift. They spurn the highest honor.

God abides in the stillness, in the hidden shadows of life, in the mundane, in the daily duties in life. Those that get quiet and take time to pray, to converse with God, develop a unique friendship with Him. God reveals Himself to the little ones of the earth.

Who is God? He is a Father. He is a Friend. He is a Creator-Artist. He is beyond your realm of thought. He seeks obedient children to love Him with abandon.

God dwells in light inaccessible. As you draw near to His light, the glow embers affect your person. Moses' face shined with God's glory after conversing with Him on the mountaintop. Even so today, God needs children with 'glory faces' to portray His light to the world.

The land is dark and foreboding. My bodies of light illuminate the world around them. They are true lighthouses of hope to a despairing and hopeless world.

Sadly, many of these glory lights are getting sidetracked by the world around them. They have lost the way of personal communication with their Friend.

Speak to them for Me. I need their time to transform them into the glorious spectacles of grace I created them to be."

Jesus,
Glory Creator for God

December 23, 2016

"The world has become a desert wasteland of souls that are barren, dry, and thirsting for water. They are dragging themselves to wells of dirty and contaminated water to quench their severe thirst. They cannot find Me in the world, even though "by Me all things consist." They have chosen to rebel against the truth, searching for strange pastures, rejecting My green pastures of holiness and peace.

Many have wandered so far from home that they cannot find their way back. Their souls are famished and hungry, yet they cannot find food to sustain themselves.

Sin is a murderer of souls. It kills, steals, robs, and destroys. Sin destroys beauty and integrity. It destroys relationships and families. It lies at the door waiting to devour the gift of life before it blossoms.

Carcasses are strewn along the roads of the world. My salvation has been rejected. How sad the hosts of heaven are! They see the scattered and desolate children on earth destroyed in rapid succession.

Who will stop this mass murdering of the souls I have created? Who will confront the dark forces controlling the world's evil system? Where are My Davids and My Gideons? They are caught up in things of no value while the desolate perish at their side.

You have the words of eternal life, My beloved ones. Share them with your dying brothers and sisters in the world. They are on the brink of soul suicide with no one to stop them. Shine My light upon them by your holy lifestyle. "Come out from among them and be separate ..." Do not join in with them. March in the opposite direction and they will follow you to the light. You are the light of the world. Shine for them."

Jesus,
Light

December 24, 2016

"I have come to set My people free. Sin has ruled for a season, but the incessant intercessory prayers of My chosen ones have borne fruit.

"This kind cometh not out but by prayer and fasting." Spiritual wickedness cannot be fought against by indulgent Christians. Prayers become powerful before My Father when they are spoken forth from a holy and undefiled life.

"The effectual, fervent prayer of a <u>righteous man</u> availeth much." In your holy living is your power to move the hand of God.

By My presence within you, you bring peace to desecrated ground. The powers over this city are mighty, but I protect My praying saints. I have raised up an army of praying and fasting souls to tear down the bars and gates erected over this city. Your part is to look to Me daily for direction, to walk humbly with your God. I will use the lowly to bring down the proud and the strong.

As the bars of Communism fell in a day, so will I batter the ramparts erected over this hallowed ground, made holy by the prayers of countless saints over the years. The history of this land has caused Satan to go on a rampage against it. He thrives in desecrating holy landmarks. He sets up his idols over them to rebel against God.

I am doing a new thing over all the land. I have raised up a leader willing to live truth. He has set his face like a flint against the falsehood and pandering that has ruled the government.

I am looking at America in the eyes of the lowly ones across the land, those trying to live righteously. Those on the fringes have ruled long enough, setting the land on fire with iniquity.

Remember your part in this, My children on earth. Live holy lives. Keep yourself unspotted from the world.

Fast and pray. Walk humbly with your God. The time is ripe to reap the harvest."

Jesus,
Warrior for God's Hosts

December 26, 2017

"Life's sadness is the road to eternity. Sin entered the world, which leads to suffering and death.

The world mourns in subjection to sin and man's willfulness. Creation groans in travail until the time of the consummation of all things.

The brightest light shines out from heaven, but man chooses to remain in darkness. Sin has become man's highest pleasure. He hides from the light, as Adam hid from God in his disobedience.

"I am the Light of the world. He that comes to Me shall not walk in darkness but shall have the light of life."

"I am all things to all men."

"Come to Me, ye that are burdened and heavy laden, and I will give you rest."

I have promised endless blessings and joy to My children on earth. I came to rescue them from darkness. I paid the price for their redemption from sin, yet they run from mercy.

All that come to Me, I will receive joyfully. I open My arms of love to them, to comfort them on their journey through life. I am here to help you, My lovely children. Come to Me to be saved.

My angels stand on guard, ready to assist My beloved children. They are startled at man's resistance to grace. They surround My faithful souls lovingly, pointing out the road to holiness and the entrance door to heaven.

Time is fleeting. Death comes quickly. Help is near. Call upon My name. I am available to all.

"Look to Me that your face may be radiant with joy." I came to give you abundant life. It is yours for the asking."

Jesus
God's Heir

December 27, 2017

"A gloomy trail is part of the spiritual journey. Clouds cover the sun and each step becomes a drudgery. These are the teaching hours – the moments you learn how to lean upon Me for everything in your existence.

You must keep walking steadily through the wind and rain, setting your face like a flint through each hardship. I walk before you, though you see Me not. The fog hides Me. I want you to learn to walk courageously and faithfully through the darkness. This increases your faith and trust.

How can you grow in blind faith in the sunny days of prosperity? God shines on you and all is well. But in the dark days when God hides Himself, do you fall apart in despair, distrusting God's plans or do you confidently trust that He is leading you through the darkness?

Life is not an easy journey. There are many mountains to climb and hills to scale. Obstacles on the path confuse and perplex you. Can you feel My presence in the darkness? I am there, awaiting your obedient response of trust.

I walked the lonely road of the cross on earth. I was troubled and perplexed by man's obstinacy; I felt burdened by other's problems and defeats; I felt helpless and the despair of darkness, yet I remained firm and steadfast, giving you an example of how to endure these trials in a way that pleases God.

I did not murmur or complain. I did not commiserate with others. I held My peace and talked everything over with My Father. I trusted Him implicitly.

I trudged wearily forward on the road, singing songs of worship in My heart. I endured, trusting in My Father's mercy.

You do the same. Rely on Me every moment and you will receive the strength you need to endure. Your obedient trust is making you mature spiritually.

Keep going forward. I am with you."

Jesus,
Encourager of the Saints

December 28, 2017

"The beauty of life is to rest in My love and will for you. It is to be content where I have placed you. It is to give thanks to God in <u>all</u> circumstances. It is to take the high road, walking with God in your daily duties.

It is not hard to walk with God. You mentally hold your hand out to Him and ask Him to lead you, to help you. God does not ask for perfection in daily living as much as a loving eagerness to please Him, to try to do the right thing at all times.

God is not a merciless taskmaster, but a loving Father willing to help you in every area of your life. Turn to Him at all times in every occurrence. You will find Him waiting there to help you. This is "humbly walking with thy God" daily.

Develop a loving relationship with the Holy Spirit. He longs to focus your life upon God and His perfect will for you. He kindly leads you in right paths and makes the way plain before you. He will show you God's perfect will if you but ask Him. He does not hide Himself from your daily activities.

He stands behind you, as it were, the voice behind saying to you, "This is the way. Walk in God's paths, which are paths of peace". He is always speaking to you, but you cannot hear Him clearly unless you get still and quiet before Him to hear His instructions.

This is the way of God. He speaks in the silence and the stillness. God hides Himself in the silence. You must seek Him out in His hiding place of peace and quiet.

Be thankful that you continue to hear My words so clearly. This is My gift to you. My merciful love has granted you an open heart. God has favored you. Rejoice in His love."

Jesus, God's Son

December 30, 2017

"To be God's friend is the highest honor on earth. To know God intimately in your life journey is pure joy.

Though the days are dark, God is beside you, helping you, guarding you, guiding you as the apple of His eye.

God delights in His friends. They are His greatest accomplishments. All creation praises God, but mankind has separated itself from his Creator.

Noah was God's friend. Enoch was God's friend. Moses was God's friend. Samuel was God's friend. David was God's friend. Isaiah was God's friend. Jeremiah was God's friend. The Bible is filled with men that cultivated a friendship with God. They walked humbly with Him. They listened for His voice. They poured their hearts out to Him. They obeyed Him. They rejoiced in their great discovery of God. They found the pearl of great price and left all to serve Him.

Things are not what they seem. The world looks glamorous and exciting, but all it offers is emptiness and meaninglessness. God in the silence offers fulfillment, peace, joy, and a heart filled with the love of heaven.

Cultivate your friendship with God as a gardener cultivates his garden. Spend time in the garden with God getting to know Him. Share your heart's intents with Him. He is a wonderful listener and is interested in everything you tell Him. He delights in you as a father dotes on His child.

Make God proud of you in the sight of the heavenly courts by being obedient and loving. Be humble and quiet, letting others go their own way.

You keep your eyes on your great Friend who loves you as no other. He loves your smiles of contentment and acquiescence to all He brings to you.

All is for your good. He is teaching you how to live in heaven where all is holy and good.

Your Friend is always by your side. Acknowledge His presence and your joy will be full."

Holy Spirit of Love

December 31, 2015

"Graces and blessings fall like raindrops upon the heads of the children that seek Me daily. These little souls quiet themselves to listen to My voice in the silence, away from the noise and distractions of life.

The world is attractive to the eyes and the ears. The pride of life is alluring and beautiful to the senses.

My wise children turn away from what is presented to their senses to seek the God of silence and obscurity in the land of faith. The door to heaven is called faith. Faith can hardly be defined, for it is a gift from God. All God's gifts are beyond definition in their grandeur.

Like the eye that can take in all things at once, faith encompasses every virtue. Faith is the arrow pointing to heaven as the goal. Faith is to believe in what you cannot see. Faith sees beyond earth's limitations. It peers into God's infinity.

Faith is your gesture of love and trust, your belief in all I have told you. Faith believes to the point of death, blindly following Christ into the shadowlands.

Faith grows in proportion to your time in My presence, for to know Me is to love Me. To love Me is to trust Me and to have faith in Me.

The more time you spend with Me, the more certain your faith, the more pure your countenance, the more peaceful your spirit and the more obedient you become.

You obey because you love. Love makes obedience a beautiful gift in response to so many gifts, the first being the honorable gift of life.

Faith tells you that I love you, that I gave My life for your love, that I am waiting for you in heaven.

Faith is the gold coin that opens the door to My Heart."

Jesus,
Faith Builder

February 5, 2018

"Be still and know that I am God." As you sit quietly in My presence, you come to know Me personally. You start to taste My goodness, to feel My great love for you. Heaven appears sweet to you and all on earth as passing.

These are the times of refreshings, the cleansing of your soul as you look upon God's holiness. You cannot remain in My presence without becoming changed in your spirit.

I abide in the depths of your soul waiting for you to acknowledge My presence. My glory lies hidden within you waiting to manifest as glorious light.

No person looking upon My face can escape the glow of My grandeur. They become radiant with My Essence. Glory rays from heaven shine around your body, touching each cell, rejuvenating each atom.

"I am the Light of the world." My light is My healing presence among you and within you. As you lay beneath My light, I radiate My holiness to you. You become transformed into My divine nature.

The world pulls you away from this radiance. It allures you to fleshly pursuits that end in dark deadness.

"The light of the body is the eye. If thine eye be single, thy whole body shall be full of light." I am the eye of your soul, the all-seeing God of the universe. As you let Me live in you in all My glory, your body becomes the lighthouse

I intended you to be, a light directing souls to Me and My world of spiritual delights.

Sit before Me quietly. See what I will do with a weaned vessel. I will fill you with light, with My joy and peace, the continual conditions of heaven, the Eternal City where I dwell among My chosen ones.

The littlest ones understand these teachings. They understand the nothingness of the temporal. They seek God alone and He bends to their lowliness.

It is all so simple. Come to Me without guile, in sincerity and love, and I will inhabit all of you, drawing you into My sacred and holy heart.

You will become light as I am Light. We will be one in purpose. Your days will become the days of heaven, for I am heaven and he who abides in Me lives heaven on earth now."

Jesus,
God Dweller Among Men

February 7, 2018

"The needs of the world are what attract My attention. I am Love; therefore, I long to give, to help, to sustain, to feed, to comfort.

Man is a feeble and needy creature. His breath can be taken away at any moment and he would fall lifeless to the ground. I have given man his life breath. I sustain that breath every moment of his existence. My love brought him into existence.

I am a God of <u>every</u> moment of your life. You are My breath, the breath of God. I exhaled you into existence. Man has no understanding when he does not acknowledge his feebleness.

When I ask you to become a little child, it is only that you might recognize your failure to thrive unless I sustain you. The humble recognize that they are but a breath exhaled from My goodness.

O, little people of earth, when will you recognize your Creator? I seek your love. I have come to earth for your love. I have condescended to nothingness for love of you.

Men of earth, you forsake your own mercy. I offer you abundant living, yet you run away from My goodness.

O, the heart of man is restless and cruel! Man fights man. Man oppresses man. Love has vanished. Only the poor and needy recognize My presence on earth.

The drama unfolds. Soon the weaver's tent will be rolled up and what is done will be done. Those that have made a covenant with Me by sacrifice will be greatly rewarded. They shall walk with Me in white, for they are worthy stewards of My gifts and graces.

Go forward, littles ones, in My grace. I shepherd you as a sheepherder tends his flock. I see all things and reward accordingly.

The littlest ones, the children, are the delight of My heart. I do not have to explain Myself to them. They love Me for who I am and for what I am to them. "Suffer the little children to come unto Me and forbid them not, for of such is the kingdom of heaven."

All will be well, My littlest ones, My flock of children. You will abide in My love forever and ever."

Lovingly,
Jesus-Child

February 9, 2018

"The song of love sung in purity and sincerity reaches My ears swiftly in My heavenly courts. My servant, David, sang Me beautiful love songs in sincerity and I took him from the sheepfolds to be king over all Israel.

David knew My heart of love. He understood My longings to be with the children of men. David listened eagerly for My whisper of love and direction. David truly was "a man after My own heart."

How difficult it is for man to put away his interests and to seek for My good pleasure. Even though I am abundant life, man has not found this treasure hidden in the field of life. It can only be found when you search for it in the silence and solitude of seeking the unseen in a world madly in search of what is seen.

To man, there is no reward or pleasure to sit silently in My presence. The flesh rebels against a discipline that seems pointless in a hyperactive world. But this is exactly where the treasure is hidden – in solitude where you will find Me waiting eagerly for you.

My voice is drowned out in your daily activities and occupations. I speak in a gentle whisper that cannot be heard in the noisy din of constant chatter and activity. To those that seek the silence, I reveal the deeper meaning of life.

In the shade, you will find your answers, not in the hot sun. Abiding beneath the branches of My presence will open your spiritual eyes to the eternal and lasting reason for your existence.

Those that plan our gentle encounters come to find that they cannot get enough of Me. They relish the peace and joy they receive when they come close to My heart.

All is well in My presence. Questions do not arise, for all is well in the soul. Then you come to understand My heart of love, so misunderstood by mankind. You see that all I can do is give beautiful gifts to My children, sometimes in the guise of trials and tribulations – gifts to heal their souls. "All things work together for good to those that love God."

Those who abide in Me, those who never leave My presence live the life of heaven even while on earth. Such great reward for so little effort!

Get quiet! "Be still and know that I am God." Be silent. Let Me speak. Leave the world of sense. Enter the world of spirit. There you will find fullness of joy in My presence.

The secret of life – live alone with God alone."

Jesus,
Harbinger of Truth

February 10, 2018

"This proclamation of faith and renouncement gladdens My heart. My desire is to form holy sons and daughters, souls of goodwill to do My good pleasure in all things. These children will rule and reign with Me forever.

You have no idea what the eternities hold. My realm is inconceivable to your finite mind. As far as your mind can roam, it will never enter your heart to understand the spiritual dimensions of eternity.

This picture is so much bigger than man's capacity to understand or believe. All these universal secrets are hidden from the wise and given to the littlest ones, My humblest children on earth, "those that truly have made a covenant with Me by sacrifice."

As you humble yourself as a little child, you begin to understand My ways. "Only the pure in heart will see God." In your purity is your understanding of what I desire from you.

Man runs ahead of Me on his own, thinking he can direct his life to his liking. He soon comes to obstacles too heavy to handle. Only then does he recognize his Creator.

"Obedience is better than sacrifice." If you obey as a little child, you will begin to understand the path of light set before you. As you learn to "come boldly before the throne of grace," My heart, life will take on a totally new dimension. Your priorities will change, your desires will change, your heart will change, your life will change.

I have called the littlest ones to Myself. "You have not chosen Me; I have chosen you." My love compels Me to condescend to your littleness.

I have a special place in My heart reserved just for you. No one can take that place. It is for you alone. My love compels Me ..."

God,
Your Father of Compelling Love

February 13, 2018

"Prayer is a universal language among all of God's holy people. It is a link between the hearts of My faithful ones. It is a golden chain linking souls together for an eternal purpose, God's blueprint for the earth.

Prayer from a sincere and pure heart is a holy language, the language of the elect in heaven. All barriers to God are broken down when a pure prayer pierces the heavens. There is a holy hush in heaven when a pure heart adores God on earth. The prayer of a child glides to heaven on the wings of an angel. Prayer draws God to hearts on earth, causing glorious rays to touch land.

The prayer God seeks is a pure and unselfish heartfelt desire to know and love God. A pure, holy, steady gaze into God's holiness purifies every sentence structure into a powerful arrow of fruitfulness for souls.

God is in His holy temple, listening to the cries of His children on earth. He hears each sigh and sees every tear. He is gentle and compassionate and responds quickly to all needs.

Life is a testing ground, a weeding out of sin from the life. All tends to purity for "only the pure in heart shall see God."

"The light of the body is the eye. If the eye be single, the whole body shall be full of light." The singleness is purity of intention towards God and man. Where duplicity reigns, God flees away to holiness.

What is holiness? A pure intention, sincerity of heart, the desire to do God's will above all things. Those that practice these gifts are precious in God's eyes and He leans down from heaven to offer His all-encompassing assistance.

God is love and He seeks lovers of Himself. Those that love God are truly blessed on earth and in heaven.

To know God on earth is the greatest and highest gift offered to mankind. It is free for the asking, but you must ask with truth in your heart."

Jesus,
God's Instructor of Holy Living

February 15, 2018

"Purity of heart, purity of intention, purity of thought, purity of speech, purity in every form all lead the soul into God's pure presence. I seek to draw pure souls into My most sacred and pure heart.

I am forming sons and daughters of purity upon earth. They shall form a circle of My intimate friends throughout the eternal ages. They loved Me above themselves through an obscure passage through life, many of them martyrs unto death. Shall I not reward these souls of purity and denial of self? I shall reward them eternally. I am forming a heavenly family to rule and reign with Me.

How important it is to take your spirituality very seriously! There is no greater task. You must keep yourself unspotted from the world, for it taints your purity. It draws you into the web of the temporal. It obscures your vision and stunts your spiritual growth.

Every day you must stay on the road I have set before you. Do not let down your guard or you could be mortally wounded by the world, the flesh, and the devil who seeks whom he may devour. This is a battle for your mind and your heart, for where your treasure is, there also is your affection and desire.

My first commandment is to love God with all your heart, soul, mind, and strength. This is your daily mission, not to let anything come in between this love for God.

To keep on track, you must be recollected and prayerful, mindful of the dangers surrounding you on all sides. You must stay in constant contact with your Lord and Savior, Jesus Christ and His Holy Spirit of support. You must have tunnel vision – God and God alone.

This is a battle for your soul. Only those who keep the weapons of prayer and sacrifice hoisted high will remain standing, those who truly have made a covenant with Me by sacrifice.

These daily rest stops with Me, listening to My voice sitting in solitude are also your weapons of warfare to grow in My image and likeness. The more time you spend alone in My presence, the more you will resemble Me in all of your life.

The way is hard but trust Me to help you. As you lean on Me, I will direct all of your paths – My promise to you. You need not fear, for I am with you in all things."

Jesus,
God's Warrior of Truth

February 19, 2018

"Rest in Me, My children. Where is your trust in My merciful love? Yes, the way is obscure, but I just ask you to take one step at a time trusting in My leading guidance.

Worry is a total lack of trust. Reasoning is also a lack of trust. "Lean not unto your own understanding ..."

I command you to "trust in the Lord <u>with</u> <u>all</u> <u>your</u> <u>heart</u>." I promised to direct your paths and I will do so. Leave worrying and reasoning behind like a worthless coat in the heat of summer. It is not needed.

As you trust in My Providential designs, you begin to live in trustful joy. You live as a child of freedom in the world, entrusting all to your Father in heaven who takes care of all things for you.

True trust is a sign of spiritual maturity in your life journey. Few souls experience a trusting spirituality. They live in fearful expectation and dwell on useless worries and fears which destroy peace and joy in daily life.

Can you offer Me these burdens and go on your way? I will let you know if you are displeasing Me. I will show you how to return to God's path and God's designs over your life.

You honor Me when you trust Me. I can serenely abide in your heart filled with peace and trust. There is no agitation and unrest to drive forth My Spirit of tranquility.

Meditate on the virtue of trust today. Ponder its meaning. Ruminate over this word until you squeeze all of its meaning out into the open pastures of your life.

Trust means no more useless worrying or reasoning. Trust brings peace.

Will you accept My peace in your life this day by trust in Me and abandonment of all that complicates your life?"

Jesus,
Perfect Truster In God

*"Your life choices follow
you into eternity."*

February 20, 2018

"The halls of heaven are filled with the cries of souls in anguish and deplorable conditions. The world is evil and full of anguish and woe.

The children are suffering for the sins of the parents. The innocent suffer the wrath of the wicked.

My eyes roam to and for throughout the earth to show Myself strong for those who trust in My help.

The convulsive nature of man erupts into a volcano of wickedness and pitiless abuse. Prayer is the only mitigating factor to hold back the tide of evil sweeping the earth.

Prayer holds back the forces of evil that seek to condemn and destroy.

The devil is triumphantly riding over men's heads in victory. Families are being destroyed, souls are bought and sold for evil purposes, holiness has vanished from the land, purity has collapsed as a virtue. If the foundations are destroyed, what can the righteous do?

God looks down from heaven to see if there are any who understand, that seek the face of God. God listens to the prayers of the just. His ears are open to their cries. He is a refuge in the day of distress to those who call upon Him and trust in His merciful love.

Have hope, My people. There is a day of reckoning and it is soon. I will divide the sheep from the goats.

I am watching, O little men of earth. My eyes see every little detail, each gesture of love, each hurtful wound. "Vengeance is Mine ... I will repay."

I will protect My little ones when they cry out to Me. Though they be bereft and burdened, I will be their help in time of trouble.

Do not be afraid. Trust in My love for you. I am God. Nothing is impossible with Me."

Your Father in Heaven Who Cares for The Littlest Lambs on Earth

February 21, 2018

"Your love for Me is what I seek above everything you could offer Me. I died for love of you. I created the world for love of you. I created you to love Me.

There are no boundaries to My love. It is continuously expanding to infinity and beyond. Mankind has no conception of the love of God. Your realm is hidden under the veil of the material world of sense. Man has not discovered the infinite spiritual world of love.

All was created for love. God is love. He can only love. Love is His Essence. Man cannot understand this.

The angels proclaim God's love unceasingly. The saints join in the holy chorus. Creation shouts out God's love. The gift of life is God's breath of love.

"Live in love, as Christ has loved you." By living in My love, you radiate My light to the world of souls walking in darkness. By living in love, you perfume the air with the scent of My love.

David played love songs on his harp that ascended on the winds to My home in heaven. I looked upon this little boy with such love in My heart that I could not but exalt him to a kingship upon earth. He truly was "a man after My own heart."

All the lovers of God that have been born have become great saints in the eyes of heaven. All their deeds were done for love of God. All their service was an outpouring of their love for God.

They imitated Jesus, God's Son, in His humility and poverty of spirit because of their love of God. They exuded God's fragrance and radiance to a darkened land. They were the lights set on a high hill that could not be hidden.

You have not chosen Me. I have chosen you because of My great love for you.

Respond as David did. He sang Me love songs. He praised My glory. God was David's life. How I long to be your life!

Where are My little David boys on earth, loving Me with every cell in their being? So few and far between.

It is a shameful thing that mankind has forgotten His loving Creator.

I seek My little souls of love to draw them into My heart, the vortex of love. They shall dwell with Me eternally in My loving embrace."

God,
Vortex of Love

February 23, 2018

"The more you give Me of yourself, the more freely I can change your life into My life. If the vessel is available and pure, I can freely enter in My holiness to cleanse, heal, lead, and guide.

As you daily seek My face, your faithfulness draws Me to you. "Draw near to God and He will draw near to you." As I become the king of your life, you start to exhibit My qualities in your person – My purity, My radiance, My joy, My light, My wisdom, My eternal being.

I came to earth to inhabit men, to live and dwell in and among them, to build a spiritual temple where I reign as Lord and God forever.

There is a small remnant of souls that seek Me in spirit and truth. As in the days of Noah, of Sodom and in the days of lone prophets exclaiming My messages to a disbelieving populace, so it is in these last days. My faithful remnant is hidden away in My heart, sending up tears and sighs for the deliverance of the nations. They are "another Christ" in the world, beseeching the Father for the salvation of the world.

Little flock, you are not alone. You are surrounded by a great cloud of witnesses. As Elijah was surrounded by the fiery chariots of heaven, so you are surrounded by praying saints from every century, praying and weeping for you to persevere in the eternal battle for lost souls. My Mother is among them, interceding for the nations.

This is no small thing, this battle for souls. The seriousness of prayer is shunned, even by some elect.

Stay strong, My remnant souls, in the power of My might. I will gird you with My strength. Do not be discouraged. The victory has been won in the heavenlies.

The battle is drawn out in array to the confusion of the principalities and powers that rule the nations. Christ-King has conquered the kingdom for God.

Satan is dismayed. This is his last effort to insult and offend God. It is a lot of noise and confusion, blustery threats, and a profusion of evil, but the end is near when Christ the King will deliver the kingdom in all His glory to the Father.

The lines are drawn up for battle. Christ-King is the head of the little ones kept unspotted from the world in purity."

Holy Spirit, Voice for Jesus

February 28, 2018

"Words of surrendering love draw Me into your heart in My fullness. I hear so few words of absolute and surrendering love.

My saints have been My greatest lovers. Their deeds proceeded from their dilated hearts of love. They did glorious works because their love compelled them to follow Me absolutely. They gazed upon My loveliness and were transformed into glorious spectacles of grace. Their faces were truly unveiled in love before Me.

I seek lovers of My heart. I seek souls to inundate and penetrate with My Person. I cannot break through the barrier of sin that surrounds rebellious souls. My holiness is repelled by evil. Only humble, lowly, obedient, and pure children have true fellowship with Me, for arrogance is odious to My holiness.

I bare My Heart to My Littlest Ones, those who look to Me for ALL. As you walk through this valley of death, I am with you as your Shepherd – leading, guiding, sustaining, feeding, and loving.

O My people, come to Me in your littleness. Allow Me to bless you, to comfort you, to be your true Father. My fatherly heart yearns to embrace every soul on earth, but so many sons are prodigals. They refuse My overtures. They run into pastures of sin. I sent My Son to rescue them, but they refuse His generous sacrifice.

What a burden this oppressed world is to Me! I long to bless them, but they run from Me. I pursue them in My mercy, waiting for the troubles of life to drive them to My merciful and fatherly embrace.

"My sheep hear My voice." They follow Me closely. They comfort My broken fatherly heart. They pray for their lost brothers and sisters to return to the fold of My love. How I love My docile, loving sheep!

Life is a short mist, over quickly. Learn from Me how to make each moment multiply into gold coins laid up for you in heaven.

Come, Littlest Ones, rest in My heart."

God,
Father of Nations

March 1, 2018

"Turbulent times are ahead for the world. I am raising up an army of souls prepared to pray the world through these tribulations and trials. These souls need to be strong in the power and strength of the Lord Jesus Christ. They will be warriors for God in enemy territory, as the hordes of demonic spirits take control of the land and men's hearts.

These days are called the last days in Scripture. Satan rules and reigns on earth in a very powerful way. Man has given him the freedom to control the environment, the political powers, the media, the entertainment world, and the souls of the innocent children by his propaganda.

Mankind will be alerted as to what lies ahead. God is a merciful Judge, not willing that any should perish but that all should come to repentance.

My remnant saints will advance against the enemy through the power of their holy lives and intercessory prayer. They shall be protected from the onslaught of the enemy as the Israelites were protected from the plagues of Egypt. They shall be quiet but powerful, hidden away from the world's activities, fighting the battle for souls in their prayer closets.

Men will be martyred by humiliations, scorn, rejection, and persecution. They will be cast out as fools. They will no longer be able to live in the world as before, because wickedness will be odious to them.

As Lot's soul was vexed in Sodom, so will My elect live out their days hidden away with Christ in God, imploring heaven to intercede for the souls of men drowned in wickedness.

The rise of homosexuality is a sign to this generation, for just as Sodom was judged for its misuse of the body for lurid practices, so this generation will be judged for trying to change the law of God.

My saints, be encouraged. I am with you. You are the apple of My eye. I have set a hedge of protection around you and your families as I did with My servant, Job. Do not fear the enemy for I stand beside you, ready to fight for you. Stand aside and see the salvation of the Lord.

Be sober as you walk through your day. Your adversary, the devil, is prowling around as a roaring lion seeking whom he may devour. Only those outside the fold of My love are vulnerable to his attacks.

You cannot afford to mingle with the world in these dreaded days. You must stay very close to Me, for the battle will be horrific."

Jesus,
Warrior

March 6, 2018

"The light that you need to understand My love for you is a grace diffused in your soul by My Holy Spirit. He is the Spirit of Love. The Holy Spirit will teach you about Me and My infinite love for you.

"Draw near to God and He will draw near to you." As you endeavor to seek Me <u>with all your heart</u>, My Spirit reveals to you that I am seeking you <u>with all My heart</u>. Let My love settle upon you and you will know the great secret of the saints, the transforming love of God that sets the world on fire.

Love drives away darkness for love is light. Light opens the spiritual eye to the eternal. As you linger here in My presence, My light opens your spiritual eyes to the reality of eternal life in My realm, a realm beyond your perception in time and space.

As you sit before Me peacefully and contentedly as the littlest child, I settle upon you in My holiness, transforming you into a child of light, transparent with heaven's light to the world.

Your prayers pierce the heavens, bringing souls into My courts for healing. As you are sanctified, you do sanctify the world around you.

Only the pure and humble shall know My ways. I reveal Myself to the Littlest Ones, the children who have humbled themselves before Me. They are the truly wise ones in this confused world. Their words of wisdom pierce the souls of the erudite. They speak the words of God to souls.

"Looking unto Jesus, the author and finisher of your faith." Jesus is the light of the world. As you proclaim "Jesus," light springs forth and God's love is disseminated throughout the world.

Make the name of Jesus the most beloved word on your lips, for there is great healing power in the name of Jesus. The world does not understand the saving power of the holy name of Jesus, the Christ, the only Son of God.

Make of the rest of your life an exhumation of the holy name of Jesus to bring life to the world. Wherever His name is breathed, life springs forth.

"By Him all things consist."

Jesus,
Life Breath

December 21, 2017

"The resurrection life is attained by few of My followers. The resurrection life is a life of complete abandonment to the will of God, a life of true trust, accepting all that happens as God's Divine Providence. It is rejoicing in tribulations, walking humbly daily with God, having eyes with an eternal perspective, and a life lived in God's merciful charity.

The world is harsh and broken. It breaks people down, causing them to become cynical and to despair.

The resurrection people walk a broad road of joyful abandonment, not bewailing their circumstances, but rejoicing in the Lord in all things.

To live the resurrection life, you must surrender everything to the Holy Spirit who lives within you. He desires to put everything in order in your life. He desires to transform you into a holy child of God, set apart for the Master's use.

He leads, guides, enlightens, and directs all your activities according to God's perfect will. He gives joy in times of sadness, peace among chaos, love in the most unlovely situations. He reveals the eternal perspective of all that occurs daily. He reveals the life of the Trinity to those who search for God's good pleasure.

The Holy Spirit is driven away by pride, evil intent, maliciousness, and a lack of mercy. He abides with the pure in heart, the chaste, those unspotted by the world, the souls that seek for truth. He desires to refashion God's children into masterpieces of love and holiness.

He makes purity evident to the world. He reveals the supernatural aspect of life. He reveals God's heart.

So few are filled with the Holy Spirit in these last days! He is available to all the sons of God but is driven away by sinful lifestyles. He only communicates Himself fully to surrendered hearts. He is God's voice to the nations.

Holiness is a mystery to the world. It is veiled grace in motion. It is pure, constant, steady, peaceful, loving, merciful, and joyful. It is strength to follow God joyfully through all life brings.

Enter the silence to beg God for the holiness of the Holy Spirit's indwelling God power."

Jesus,
God's Broadcaster

March 7, 2018

"All of nature is a book of life to men. Nature is subject to My will in all things. Nature moves at My command. Nature does not rebel or revolt against Me or My authority.

Nature is a beautiful and transparent picture of God. Varied, glorious, made of the finest particles, the trees sway lovingly back and forth in humble docility before My majestic presence. The ocean shines and sparkles with My movement, ever changing, ever new. The clouds drift in a convoluting pattern over the earth, protecting and sheltering mankind.

The animal kingdom is subjugated to man's judgment in all things. All of nature is at man's disposal. He can preserve it or destroy it. He can nourish the trees or cut them down. He can smell the fragrant air or pollute it with chemicals. He can enjoy swimming in My oceans or he can throw tons of refuse into the beautiful turquoise water.

I have put the earth into the hands of man. I have given man dominion over the animal and plant kingdoms. This is the garden I have planted for man's domain, My gift of love to him. My heart is wounded when I see My gifts destroyed mercilessly.

O men of earth, can you not appreciate the beauty of your planet, so delicately created by My loving hands? Can you not rejoice in the dazzling array of colors, sights, and sounds that I have so mercifully given to you? Can you not take special care of My beautiful gifts of love that I have given you to safeguard?

Can you not treat My animals with thanks and loving respect? Each animal is a reflection of My love for this planet and the men and women I have created so marvelously.

Come into My presence with thanksgiving for I have bountifully blessed you, My children. All I'm asking is that you tenderly care for the things of earth I have entrusted to you. They are My beautiful gifts of love to you. Do not trash them unmercifully.

My heart is wounded within Me. This generation has shunned My gifts in abandon. You have chosen concrete and clay over heavenly substances.

The earth will revolt at this inhumane treatment. I have willed it so."

God,
Judge of Man's Indifference
Toward His Gifts

March 7, 2018

"Sitting here with Me in this empty church is a beautiful act of love that you offer in homage to Me. The world calls you to more important things, but you have discovered the all-important secret to all existence, spending time in intimacy with your Creator and Friend.

I have so few friends in the world, true friends that give of their time willingly to Me. So many of My children are busy, too busy to spend time needed in My presence, the time it takes to develop a true friendship.

I have called you here. "You have not chosen Me; I have chosen you." You have responded to my choice in love. "Many are called, but few are chosen" because so few respond to My calls of grace.

The world's cries are urgent and dominant. The world has many responders and true followers, showing their allegiance daily. Where are those allegiant to Me, responding promptly to My loving invitations to friendship, a life walking humbly with your God?

Grace calls unceasingly, crying out in the streets, lingering among the sick beds, lovingly standing by in loss and sorrow. My grace is the strength of the saints in glory, the magnificent sustenance of the saints on earth.

Mercy, grace, and peace call out loudly to the souls on earth offering peace, joy, and strength available to all.

The invitation is eternal, never taken back, given by an unchanging God.

"Grace, mercy and peace, from God the Father and our Lord Jesus Christ." Words of promise and hope to My chosen ones.

I am yours for the taking, sons and daughters. Come to Me as a child to a loving and generous father. I will never turn you away.

I will cover you with My robe of righteousness and crown you with the crown of a King's heir.

"Suffer the children to come unto Me ..."

Jesus,
Child Gatherer for God

March 8, 2018

"The beauty of a soul in love with God radiates a rainbow of emotions in the hearts of those who behold it. Deep in man's center is a thirst for the infinite, a quest for the eternal which he will not find among the temporal things around him on earth.

To come into the presence of a holy soul in love with God is an enlightenment to the soul. Light springs out of darkness. Sweet peace encompasses the atmosphere. Something has changed in the heart of the beholder.

God lives in pure and holy souls. Created souls sense His presence when He is allowed to manifest Himself through a purified vessel.

The glory of God, which was hidden from the Israelites, is revealed through a human body. It is ethereal and there are no words to describe the soul's workings. Something lights up in the soul and the seeker seeks to unlatch the door to these glimmering sensations. He yearns to be satisfied in his innermost being. Roaming through life, he comes up empty.

But the depths of God call to his spirit in subtle ways – a word, a gesture, an emotion, a coincidence. He gravitates to this beauty of holiness – God showing up physically on earth.

To see God in a soul is to experience the vision of life in heaven.

God has united Himself to man. Divinity took the form of humanity, for Jesus, the Son of Man, is truly God in the flesh. Jesus promised man that He would abide in him sealed with the eternal seal of the Holy Spirit.

"Christ in you, the hope of glory." Who could believe such a wonderful mystery?

"With God all things are possible," even turning bread into His actual flesh.

Will there be faith on earth to believe these things when I return?"

The Trinity Mystery

March 9, 2018

"The power of a holy life is saturated in solitude, gentle contemplation, silence, and loving prayer. To sit quietly alone with Me opens the ears of your heart to My voice within you.

You have weaned yourself from the noise of the world to listen to My silent language of love hidden within your spirit. My words of eternal wisdom can penetrate your being as they are released from the prison of your humanity to soar in the heavenly realms with Me. You are able to fly quickly to the top of the mountain realms with Me. You are able to fly quickly to the top of the mountain where I reside in holiness. The peaceful atmosphere in My presence lets you know that all is well.

What is the secret to a beautiful life? To become God's friend. How do you become God's friend? By loving Him. How do you love Him? By spending time in His presence.

God is Joy and those that spend time with Him become joyful. God is Peace and those that spend time with Him become peaceful. God is charming ad gracious, patient and benevolent, kind and thoughtful, forgiving and forgetting offenses, all-wise, and glorious.

To be a friend of God is a beautiful way to live life on earth. Your horizons become infinite. Your earthly boundaries are lifted, for "all things are possible with God."

"Come away with Me, My beloved" as I carry you to another realm of spirit where the air sparkles with holy goodness, where the music penetrates your being in a new way, where all is peace, joy, and rest. Your eyes will be opened to the beauty of My glories for ages to come.

This is the land of God, where holiness resides. No sin enters this land; only love and understanding, peaceful acceptance, and quiet joy.

In the silence I carry you away to this holy land of love. There is no other way to enter but in silent contemplation and surrender to the Holy Spirit's drawing power within you.

I am waiting for you in the inner depths of your heart. Will you come to be with Me?"

Jesus,
Your Love and Your Life Breath

March 12, 2018

"There will be gray days in your spiritual life as in your earthly life. These are days of patience and thanksgiving, taking all from God's hand in submissive surrender.

Life truly is a tapestry of contrasting threads. In your perseverance is your salvation. "They that persevere to the end shall be saved."

Above the clouds the sun is shining. Nothing has changed in God's plan, though your emotions perceive things differently. Live each day in humble obedience to My will, enduring patiently all the dark days of tribulation, testing, and sorrow.

Life will appear mundane on these gray days, but to God, these changes test your love for Him. He is training children to be saints in His kingdom.

Each child has a unique path to purify his soul. Trust and self-surrender make the path easier and more joyful.

Lack of trust breeds resentment, oppression, and fear. Lack of trust is the result of keeping your eyes away from My eyes, of turning away from the Source, your intimacy and friendship with Me. Each slight turn away from Me drags your spirit down until it no longer sees the goal of life clearly – eternity In My presence in blissful love. When your eyes are locked on My eyes, My glory reveals your destiny and you then stay the course willingly and eagerly.

You are on a spiritual journey. You must keep moving to arrive at your homeland.

If you linger on the roads of earth, you miss the great spectacles of My marvelous surprises in your life. I can make a saint out of the greatest sinner. I can bring joy amidst the greatest sorrow. I can tear down mighty bridges of evil with the slightest whisper.

I hide behind the veil of everything in your life. Every occurrence is preordained by My infinite wisdom. As you acquiesce to my workings in your life, you will experience the peace of a free and untroubled heart, the joy of heaven, and the love of God. What could be greater on earth?

Peace of heart is a coveted jewel rarely found in human souls. I am the peace they seek, but they run elsewhere, avoiding My love.

On this gray day, be confident of the sun shining above the clouds. Walk in the joy of our friendship, for all is passing until you reach the final destination – ETERNAL DAY."

Jesus,
The One Who Passed Into the Heavens Before You

March 14, 2018

"Moments of quiet reflection should be planned in advance. You will not spend time alone with Me in the spiritual realm without a strong effort to fight against the demands of life. Life wraps its tentacles around you, squeezing out peaceful meditation and reflection.

To rest quietly in My presence is very foreign to My children on earth. They thrive on achievement and activity. It is a heroic effort to sit silently, soaking up My life without any visible signs. Those that find this pearl of great price enjoy heavenly peace and godly wisdom.

To seek the face of God is your highest priority, the end for which you were created. To seek My face, you must gaze upon Me in silence, humbling your earthly members to obey you.

Men run away from quiet reflection and solitary meanderings. Man feels a void when there is no noise and the distractions cease. If he can get past the initial emptiness, the rolling meadows of heaven will manifest the heavenly rest I have destined him for.

A holy person is a quiet person, a soul weaned from endless activity and noise. There is a tranquility and an orderliness of character that is beautiful to behold. He reflects My beauty and glory. Souls sense the odor of an other-worldly perfume which attracts the good and repels the bad.

Walk purely before Me daily, seeking My face, basking in My presence, believing all that I have promised you.

Again I say to you: Do not look for the bombastic, for I am not in the earthquake. I am the silent, subtle, whispering voice behind you saying: "This is the way. Walk ye in it."

Jesus,
Voice of God

January 25, 2018

"Words convey My thoughts to you. As you listen, you understand. All is not as it seems. Wisdom will show you the way.

Stay on the holy highway, the road of the redeemed, those struggling as you are. The way is not easy; it is arduous and draining. It is the royal road of the cross. My cross bearers follow Me in procession across the centuries of time. Each has a unique cross, a sorrowful burden to bear throughout life. Only those focused on God bear their crosses gloriously.

There is no promise of an easy way. All cross bearers suffer. Their greatest anguish is to displease God in their suffering. Many burdens obscure the path. Tears blind the eyes. It is easy to veer off the road.

You must keep your hand clasped within the hand of Jesus to endure valiantly. He is the Way, the Truth, and the Life you need to emulate.

Call out to Him in your grief. He is there to guide you. He will never leave you or forsake you. He is your life breath. You were created for Him. By Him all things consist."

Holy Spirit,
Whisperer of God's Secrets

December 19, 2016

"A heart willing to be led is a joy to My heart. That is what trust is – willing to be led anywhere blindly by God who only has your best interests at heart.

I do not ask for the spectacular. I ask for a humble willingness to be led and to obey My requests. All My requests of you are directed to your sanctification. Look to Me moment by moment and let Me lead you.

To be still in My presence is still an area that you should cultivate. It will bring you peace and joy beyond your understanding. All the rushing dissipates your purpose. At the end of your life, you will realize that all the rushing around meant nothing. It was in the quiet moments that your spirit was fed and grew.

"Come to Me, all ye that are burdened and heavy laden, and I will give you rest." Let Me teach you how to rest in My love for you. It will be a new life experience. Your tensions will fall away, and you will see a new world through My eyes."

Jesus,
Rest Taker

January 28, 2016

"There is true heavenly joy when you stop to rest in God's love. So few souls know how to enter My rest. You must come away from the world. You must quietly sit before Me to seek My quiet presence.

The world has souls in its grip. They cannot flee from the power of the earth around them, yet their spirits were created for another realm, the quiet, invisible realm of spirit where God resides in silent peace and rest.

Many souls flee from the world by entering convents. They see no other way to run from the distractions surrounding and choking them in the world and its environments.

They have chosen the spirit over the flesh. They have realized that there must be a real breaking from the bondage of the flesh and its desires. They seek "the best part", to live alone with God alone, adoring Him in spirit and in truth.

It takes great courage to make this break from the world, but it is an entrance into the peaceful pastures of peace, love, and joy, a bliss unknowable by earth's inhabitants. Only the courageous enter these realms of God's abode, the spiritual realms beyond earthly thought.

You must lose your life on this earth to find your eternal life.

It seems to be a vague, obscure door beyond which you cannot see what awaits you, but if you dare to cross this threshold, you will find God lovingly awaiting you.

He stands beyond the door, waiting to see who will be brave enough to despise the earth and all fleshly delights in order to buy the pearl of great price, oneness with his Creator.

So few souls enter this heavenly life!"

February 6, 2017

"It is so simple yet so true that intimacy with your God is to be sought above all things. Life is a race, a course set for heaven. Very few finish the race in victory. They give up along the way. Think of this. Centuries upon centuries have elapsed, yet how many saints have been canonized? There are many unsung saints, yet there should be more people that have sought the highest calling in Christ Jesus.

It is not an easy road to take up your cross to follow in My footsteps, but the reward is beyond your comprehension. It is a daily battle of the will and the senses.

You must fight manfully every day of your life because you will be inundated by distractions and sensual thinking, the senses seeking to be gratified during your earthly journey.

The ascetics have learned the secrets to holiness. They have denied their bodies to live in the Spirit's embrace. They have lost their lives in this world to obtain an eternal inheritance, the glory of My presence eternally.

You have many friends in heaven praying for you. They want you to keep your eyes on Jesus, your Mediator. They want you to finish your course with joy, to hear My "Well done, thou good and faithful servant."

Subdue your earthly desires. Think of heaven. All sacrifice will be worth it when you see Jesus.

"Redeem the time because the days are evil."

Holy Spirit, Voice of God

April 1, 2017

"Grace is My free gift to you, merited for mankind by My passionate death on Golgotha's Calvary. Grace poured out from the blood in My wounded side, the cleansing flow of the blood of a God-Man, shed for the sins of the world. This blood is rejected, blasphemed, and ridiculed.

God descended to a human level to die for His children. What greater love could be comprehended! Yet this great and loving God is rejected and spurned by His children.

God's beautiful gifts, the world and its beauty and the gift of life, have been chosen over God Himself. Man has chosen what is created over his Creator. What foolishness!

Creation displays God's magnificence, God's beauty, and God's love. Creation is the cord to draw you into the heart of the beautiful God that so lovingly gives and gives.

The desire of God's heart is to be loved by His children. He longs to gather His obedient children around Him to lavish His love upon them. There is no substitute for God's love. It is thrilling.

Open your heart to allow God to love you. He longs for you to understand His heart of love. He molds His children into beings that will be able to understand and love Him. He trains His children in the ways of holiness.

Let yourselves be led, My little ones. The littlest ones know My heart."

Jesus, God's Littlest Son

June 10, 2015

"Redeem the time because the days are evil." The sands in the hourglass are running out. You cannot hold time in your hand. It races past you so swiftly. It does not turn around in its path. It runs away from you. It runs ahead of you. You cannot touch it or hold it back.

Each soul is allotted a segment of time. How you live during this space of time will be required of you by your Creator.

How do you spend your time? As you look back over the years of your life, was your time well spent?

One day you will have to give an account for the gift of time, how you have lived these few years on earth.

You have today to make the necessary changes in your life to make sufficient and eternal use of your future sands in time."

Jesus,
Time Creator

June 22, 2015

"The storm clouds hover in the sky while the thunder rumbles and the lightning makes cracks across the sky. Nature trembles when it sees My majesty and power in the heavens. My storms have become commonplace to man. He no longer sees or understands the things beyond his grasp. There is no more awe or reverence for My bounty in nature's dramas. I thunder from the heavens. I hurl lightning bolts to the earth. I crash, and I warn, and I frighten the animals with My power, yet still I am ignored by My selfish children.

An uneducated and simple man has more reverence and awe than a learned scholar. Learning has made man proud and arrogant. He has made formulations and equations for all the majestic occurrences on earth. He explains nature's rhythms with his mathematical equations and high-sounding words, yet he knows so very, very little about the power of My omnipotence. Like a proud rooster he struts on the stage until his life breath is gone. His books lie around him while men praise his accomplishments. Yet he has never looked into the heart of his Creator for the real answers to life.

Man, in his pride, has rejected His Father-Creator. Nothing could be sadder on earth!"

Jesus,
Sad for Souls

June 28, 2015

"Life is a series of beginnings and endings. The path veers off in different directions according to My Father's will. It is your task to stay on course in complete willingness and trust. You are not guiding the ship; God is. You must acquiesce to the various disturbances, sacrifices and circumstances of daily living, maintaining a serene equilibrium which is nothing other than complete trust and abandonment.

How carefree your life could be if you put all your trust in the Guide of your life! You could rejoice in every mundane occurrence, knowing that all is working together for good in your regard.

At this late stage of the game, the ending days of your life, can you spend them in serenity and trust? Can you joy in the wonders of your God? Can you appreciate all He has done for you throughout your life? Can you sing an appreciative love song as you go about your days?

Planning and worrying are wasting the precious hours that could be spent in joy-filled living. In heaven, no one is worried. There is complete trust; therefore, the singing is incessant. A cheerful, contented heart sings like a bird daily.

Your heavenly Father loves you and has given you all good things to enjoy. Show your appreciation by singing melodies in your heart unto the Lord."

Jesus,
Singer's Joy

July 8, 2015

"You are trying to serve Me and only one thing is necessary and that is your love for Me. When you love someone, they become your continual focus. Your heart is so drawn to them that life fades away around you. Each contact throws more kindling on the fire.

Lovers make time for each other. They talk, dream, and express their souls to each other. They become united as one in purpose. As your love for Me grows, life's distractions dissipate slowly. Your interests in the world slowly grow dim as you reach out to the eternal sunrise.

Your love for Me grows when you think of Me, spend time in My presence, lift your eyes and your heart up to Me, and when you say, "I love You, my Jesus." These are diamond drops to My ears. Love pulls Me to you so forcefully when you express your love to Me. "Jesus, Mary, I love You! Save souls!" The mantra of the Littlest Ones is music to My ears. Speak this until it becomes your second nature.

Every time you speak My name, I shower My blessings and graces upon your soul. Each word of love is an encapsulated rainbow of glory that I will adorn you with forever.

Love Me and life will become the greatest adventure you could ever dream of, for I am the Author of life and I know all the secrets of the Godhead where pure joy reigns."

Jesus,
Rainbow of Glory

*"If only souls knew what
joy holiness brings!"*

October 1, 2017

"Battles are expected to be fierce and troubling. It is constant warfare to remain alive. The Christian life is a spiritual battle, constantly fighting against the evil powers in this world.

Many have laid down their arms and have joined the enemy's camp. It was easier to surrender than to be constantly wounded in battle. Few soldiers are standing at the front-line defending holiness.

If you desire to live a holy life in a sinful world, be prepared to battle all the days of your life. You will be constantly shelled by the enemy. He seeks to discourage you. He wants you to give up in defeat and join the crowds of pleasure seekers that have lost sight of eternity.

Although wounded psychologically and spiritually, you must rise to your feet in My strength, keeping your eyes on the prospect of heaven and eternal rewards. Only those that persevere to the end win the prize of eternal life.

Determine to seek the eternal in all things. Let the temporal fall behind you as you race ahead to the eternal shores.

Be one of the few left standing at the end of the age, the spiritual heroes that have carried the flag of Jesus Christ boldly throughout the centuries.

Come to Me daily to be strengthened for battle.
Clothe yourself in My righteous garments.

   You cannot fight on your own without My protection.
Let Me win the war through you."

Jesus,
Captain

December 21, 2016

"Jesus, Savior, pilot me across the rolling waves of life's stormy seas. The thick night surrounds my clay vessel, but I trust that You are at the helm. Though the light has faded, I entrust the darkness to you. You are my light."

These words are beautiful to My ears. My children of faith in the world, tossed about on earth by the winds and waves, trust Me with their short journey on earth. My hand of mercy follows them all the days of their lives.

I am God. You can hear Me in the silence. Silence is My eternal language. Vistas unfold in the silence.

Be patient and wait for My voice. You will hear it. Only the patient seeker receives the reward of My Presence."

February 22, 2018

"Heaven is a place of brilliant light, joyful music, and serendipitous beginnings. The souls of the just are clad in bodies of light, each star differing in glory. Earthlings become heaven dwellers, resting in a realm of endless beauty and soundless peace.

I want to take you on a journey to your home in heaven, the place I have prepared for you in My Father's City of Light.

Souls on earth do not think of heaven. It is an ethereal dream of landscapes in the mind, yet heaven is very real and even now it is flowing with the joy and praises of My saints in light.

Why is heaven so different from earth? There is a great dividing wall between earth and heaven. Sin has built the wall. The decay of earth cannot possess heaven.

Myriads upon myriads of angels dwell with Me in glorious array. They vibrate with My glory. They are obedient and loving spirits watching over My children.

Each angel was uniquely created to show forth a particle of God's glory. As each human is unique, each angel is unique."

February 23, 2018

"I am truly here in all My magnificence, splendor, and glory hidden under the appearance of a humble piece of bread, wheat beaten and ground, for love of My people. I chose the lowest place, the hidden beauty of humility, to come to you that believe.

Here is heaven upon earth, the residence of the Creator of the universe. The monstrance is My home on earth, allowing souls to gaze on My earthly glory, to be transformed from glory to glory.

My rays of holiness embrace each soul sitting before My presence. It is a great grace to have been called here to appear before Me. "You have not chosen Me; I have chosen you." Only My merciful love could have opened your heart to the beautiful realm of Spirit. My littlest children kneel contentedly before Me soaking in My purity and radiance.

Your gazes of love pierce My most tender heart. How I love My Littlest Ones, My children of hope. I have called you to Myself "for such a time as this." This is all part of My divine plan known from eternity to eternity with no beginning and no end.

I will reveal Myself to all of you throughout the endless ages before you. You shall rejoice forever in My presence."

Jesus,
Joy of the Ages

March 5, 2018

"The name of Jesus will lift your heart to heaven, no matter the circumstances.

The prayer of Jesus will heal the sick and raise the dead in spirit to newness of life.

The herald of the name of Jesus will be filled with the anointing power of the Holy Spirit.

The fragrance of Jesus changes the face of the soul.

The presence of Jesus transforms the atmosphere.

The joy of Jesus rejoices the angelic hosts.

The remembrance of Jesus cleanses the soul from sinfulness and pride.

Give the world Jesus.

Souls need Jesus. He is the Savior of the world.

Give souls Jesus."

March 15, 2018

"Days of tedious toil and learning produce a harvest of holiness in a persevering soul of goodwill. The way of the cross is narrow, and few souls remain steadfast on the road. Life's distractions veer them off course. They waste years in fruitless endeavors. Those that stay on the royal road reap an abundant harvest of holy fruits in due time if they faint not.

Life is a race to God's kingdom. In a race, many lag behind and many drop out.

It takes steadfast endurance to continue on day after day amid struggles and disappointments, but those who keep their eyes on God will stay safely on the road. Those that rely on God's strength and power will finish the course with God's strong approval.

Now is the time of testing before the eternal banquet. "Now is the day of salvation..."

"Many are called but few are chosen ..." Those few remain steadfastly connected to God daily. They read His word; they pray; they rely on His strength; they obey His inspirations; they praise and glorify Him by a holy life.

This life is extremely short. Beg God to grant you the grace of holy perseverance, for it will be worth it all when you see Jesus, the Light of the world.

Cling to Jesus daily. Call upon Him when you are falling. Beg Him for mercy. Remember His name in the night seasons. He will assist you speedily.

He is the great Comforter sent from God to assist you on your journey. "He will never fail you or forsake you." "He is all things to all men."

"Looking unto Jesus, the Author and Finisher of our faith..."

How He loves His children struggling to please Him in the world!

Trust in His merciful love. He will rescue you in the appointed day and then your tongues shall rejoice eternally."

Holy Spirit,
Teacher of God's Loved Ones

March 17, 2018

"My love for you is God-Love, infinite love beyond your finite understanding. You yearn for Me but do not understand My infinite yearnings for you.

I created you to love you eternally. I carefully designed you in every aspect of your character. It was thrilling for Me to place a gentle spirit within your earthly body. I watched you grow, hovering over you to protect you. I knew that one day you would blossom into a beautiful flower in My garden, eager and joyous to love Me and to glorify My Father.

From your earliest moments on earth, My eyes of mercy have followed your going. I knew you would go through some very hard years, but they were learning experiences, needful for you to appreciate My paths of peace in this agitated and nonbelieving world. I have plans for your life that were in place long before your arrival to earth.

I ask My children to die to themselves, to be that grain of wheat falling into the earth to die, so that I may accomplish My perfect plan for their existence.

You have yearnings and desires that were implanted in your spirit, gifts and talents to gift the world, and a perfect path to run joyously into My eternal kingdom.

Entrust yourself completely to Me daily. Let Me run your life in every area. Turn to Me for direction in every decision.

Spend your life loving Me and you will be happy beyond your wildest dreams, for happiness is loving God in this world.

True joy is loving God with all your heart. This is spirituality. If you live your life loving God, everything else falls into place.

This is why you were created – to love Me. In this holiness consists – loving your Creator with every fiber of your being.

I have called you to Myself. I have allured you and brought you into the wilderness to speak to your heart. As you gaze upon my loveliness you begin to understand My heart, smitten for love of you.

Love Me, My dearest child. That's all I ask of you."

Jesus,
Your Love

March 18, 2018

"Do not be discouraged by your assessment of your seemingly very slow spiritual progress. I do not see your life as you see it. Your mind has an earthly veil, hiding the true spiritual riches in your soul.

I have been sifting you through these years, refining you as gold is tried in the fire. I am slowly burning away the impurities in your nature, readying you for your final journey to your homeland.

God's measure is vastly different than man's limited comprehension. God's values are diametrically opposed to the standards of man on earth. God is Spirit. Only Spirit matters define His judgments. The flesh is the means to define the spiritual efforts.

I value an obedient, humble heart above all things. Sincerity of intention, purity, and simplicity in all you do brings great joy to My heart. I know your weaknesses, your faults, your confusion. I take all things into account, for I am a just Judge, judging and measuring all things with infinite wisdom.

Trust My judgment over your own flawed perceptions. I am leading you and will point out everything that is displeasing to My holiness. Please be content with all that I allow to occur in your life. Your trust in My judgments comforts My heart.

I look upon My trusting children with such predilection. They are the apple of My eye.

The journey seems long, but it is quite short in the light of eternity. Stay the course peacefully, content to let Me have My way with you. In your contented gaze is your peace.

"All things work together for good to those who love God."

Jesus,
Lover of Your Soul

March 19, 2018

"My paths are pleasant and peaceful. When you stray from My directive will, your soul will feel troubled. When you walk in peace of soul, know that you are following My will obediently. I will not deceive you.

I have the eye of a watchful shepherd, always keeping My sheep safe. Roads can be very perilous in your Christian journey because many times what is best is not chosen over what is good. Even evil can masquerade as good.

Man harbors much self-love that colors his thinking. That is why it is so important to ask for My guidance and direction in every circumstance of your life. When you run ahead of Me instead of following Me, much time is lost, and you could fall into some perilous ditches. Then you will call upon Me to rescue you which, of course, I will, but it is better to avoid these mistakes.

You will enjoy much peace if you consult Me before you do anything in life. Your intent should be to glorify God in whatever you do.

I will show you the path to glorify God. Allow Me to be the only voice you listen to at the beginning of the day and continue in this listening spirit when you lay your head on your pillow each night. Even in the night seasons I instruct your spirit.

You are so dear to Me. If only you know how much joy you give Me.

All I desire is to raise obedient, loving, listening, joyful children, sons and daughters that make Me proud. There is such beauty in obedience.

My saints are beautiful in My eyes and gloriously beautiful to the angels and saints in heaven. How proud we are of all of you, children of God on earth!"

Jesus,
Joyful Brother

March 21, 2018

"If you seek to broaden your horizons to be able to see with an eternal perspective, then you must earnestly strive daily to keep your gaze upon God. In His time, He will grace you with many gifts and graces beneficial to your salvation and the sanctification of others.

You must come into God's presence daily and faithfully entreat Him to bless you with His divine nature. He is your Teacher and all that happens is His classroom. You have to sit patiently daily in class, absorbing His knowledge, learning His ways, growing in His grace.

Life is a process and spiritual life is an eternal process. You will be growing spiritually throughout the endless ages of eternity.

"Ye have not, because ye ask not." Those that beg daily on My doorstep receive the most food morsels. I cannot step outside the house without tripping over them. They keep themselves ever in My mind by their continual mindfulness of My presence. They flock themselves around My doorway, waiting patiently for Me to appear in all My glory. They neither need nor want anything else because they have found endless life, light, and love in their intimacy with Me. They live with Me daily, walking in peace throughout their daily duties.

One day they will cross the threshold of the doorsill to enter My heavenly home forever. They will be eternally satiated with My goodness, but until then they patiently and eagerly await My daily ration for them, as a shepherd daily feeds his flock. They do not seek great things for themselves. They enjoy being one of the flock, content to share My bounties.

How few lock eyes with Mine in this world! My flock is tiny compared with the world's population. My remnant souls follow Me wherever I lead them, contentedly grazing in My green pastures of loving sustenance. They are like little birds that are handfed by the fingers of a loving Master.

Little flock, how I love and care for you! I never forget you for a moment. You will always be the pupil of My eye, a very sensitive spot to be. I cannot see past you, for you are always within My range of vision.

Keep yourselves there, My little ones, and you will be greatly blessed by Me and by My loving Father."

Jesus,
Lover of the Sheep

March 29, 2018

"The days of earth seem long and dreary, mundane and purposeless at times, but they are your training ground in the school of holiness. Each soul has a unique course in the history of the world, a training in the arts of purity, humility, brotherly love, and respect and honor to God.

Nothing is insignificant in your daily life. Souls are always looking for the extraordinary happenings in life, whereas I work most effectively in the ordinary daily duties of each soul.

Faithfulness to duty, faithfulness to family, faithfulness to friends and strangers are beautiful virtues in the eyes of God. Heroic deeds come to you rarely in life because God dwells in the little moments that are extremely significant in terms of eternal growth in holiness of life.

You will be growing spiritually forever. It will never end, for God is infinite. He has no boundaries to end the journey of the infinite spiritual understanding of who He is.

God has chosen to raise the weak, little things on earth to the highest level of praise, for God is humble. God seeks out the humble souls for refreshment and fellowship. He delights to reveal Himself to them. They are his chosen ones on earth, beloved sons and daughter of a loving Father.

As always, I tell you: Stay the course. Keep your gaze fixed on Me. Don't listen to your emotions clamoring for your attention.

By faith, walk forward in confidence toward the Father Who lovingly watches over you constantly. He works all things together for your good. Trust that He is watching you, leading you, guiding you, and directing you every moment of your life. There will be no confusion or discouragement if you keep lifting your eyes to Me for My approval.

Remember, this is a journey, a pilgrimage. Your homeland in heaven is your final resting place. You were not created for earth, but for heaven. That is why you yearn for so much more in your spirit. That is to be expected of a pilgrim. A wayfarer is homesick for his country, constantly seeking to hasten the journey.

I am the Conductor of the train you are riding to your homeland. Trust that I know the way home and I will get you there safely.

Enjoy the ride!"

Jesus
Journey Planner

March 30, 2018

"There is so much you do not know. When souls stand on the edge of eternity and are faced with the revelation of all life's subtleties, their minds are open to the revealed truth that all created things are objects of God's love.

Love is the filter through which God views everything and it is His desire to share this love with the souls He has created. To have eyes of love in every situation is to see the world as God sees it. He compassionately ponders His creation, knowing that all is working together according to His glorious will.

Man is restless. He does not have God's peace in his heart. He does not trust that God is in control of all things. He does not have faith to believe God's promises. This is the source of his disillusionment and despair.

To have the mind of Christ, you must know that you are a child lovingly carried through life by a kind Father Who has your best interests at heart. Abandonment to God is the foundation of perfect peace in this life.

Can you truly hand your life over to God unreservedly and with complete abandonment? Can you give Him your plans and agendas instead of trying to work things out yourself and running ahead of Him? Can you trust Him daily instead of second guessing and worrying?

A child is peaceful and carefree. That is the way God wants all His children on earth to be, regardless of their age.

Man grows up on his own and feels no need for God's watchcare. He enters a world of his own making which brings empty promises and shattered dreams at the end of his life. If he had not stepped away from God, his life would have been lived in great peace and he would have died in great peace. He chose to walk away from God's ordained path for him.

Become a little and dependent child again. Smile, sing, and be at peace. Leave all your concerns and worries in My hands. I am taking care of all things in your regard.

Skip through this day in joyous abandon. Choose the joy of walking with Me today."

Lovingly,
God,
Your Loving Father

March 31, 2018

"Another day has been given to you. Each day is a gift from My Father's kind heart. My Father is a perennial gift giver. His existence is to give, for He is Love. That is the message I came to earth to display – God is love. I came to earth because of His great love for mankind.

Every day He waters the earth to make it fertile, feeds the lowly animals, makes the wind cleanse the air, shines the sun on the plants to make them grow. He rejoices in the beauties of nature, the docility of the animal world, the wonder of life in the newborn baby, and the rising of men after deep struggles. God watches the mother care so tenderly for her baby.

God sees Himself in what He has created. He sees the probing minds that seek out the mysteries of the universe, the doctors compassionately responding to the needs of the sick, the mundane worker bees, laughing and enjoying lives in poverty.

The world is a great wonder to behold when seen from God's birds-eye viewpoint. He sees all things at once; therefore, He can say: "What I have created is good."

God's bounteous generosity is seen everywhere the eye can span or the mind can think. All things have an eternal rhythm in His mind. He sees the end before the beginning and the inside before the outside. Man cannot possibly understand God's designs.

O men of earth, stand in awe and rejoice at such a loving Father-Creator. He has eternal plans for your life. Things do not end on earth. They carry on throughout the endless and bountiful eternal ages where hope becomes certainty.

God has given you so much and asks so little of you in return. He asks you to love Him with all of your heart, all of your soul, all of your strength, all of your mind. If you do this, He will take care of all the rest.

If you can focus your life on loving God, you will become the saint you desire to be. Love is the magic potion to lift you to heaven in an instant of time.

Love and all will be well. There is no higher aim than to love God with all of your being. He created you of dust, but when He put His love upon you, you became a living soul."

Jesus,
Lover of God

April 4, 2018

"My Spirit can flow through a clear vessel. There are many obstacles to the Spirit's entrance - attachments to created things, the pride of life, earthly ambitions. The vessel is so full of the things of earth that there is no room for the Holy Spirit to enter. He remains outside, unable to help, unable to counsel and guide.

The Holy Spirit is gentle and peaceable. He does not intrude or make an unwelcome entrance. He seeks peace, purity, and holiness in a heart. He seeks a soul emptied of self, waiting silently for His entrance.

To die to self is to come alive in the Holy Spirit. "Unless a grain of wheat falls to the earth and dies, it remains alone." If it dies to self's demands, it bears much spiritual fruit.

Death to self is a letting go of all that you presume yourself to be – perceptions, preoccupations, surmisings and reasonings.

It is to lie still to let God and His light penetrate your spirit. You must lie still beneath His touch. You must acquiesce to all of His promptings within you. You must say 'yes' to all He asks of you.

God is not a hard taskmaster. He is a loving and gentle Father. He seeks to guide you with a Father's leading hand. He desires to bless you, to comfort you, to grant you graces beyond your highest imaginings.

These treasures from heaven are rarely given to souls on earth because the ground soil in the heart is not prepared. It is covered with weeds and earthly debris. He cannot work freely.

Children, if you will clear out all the clutter in your lives, you will find My peace, My freedom, and My joy. Life will take on a new brilliancy. The mundane will become a stepping-stone to eternal glory.

Come out of the darkness, My children, and step into My light. Turn from evil and wickedness to embrace holiness and purity. Keep watch over your senses that the clutter of earth will not impede your spiritual journey.

Allow My sweet Holy Spirit to have His way with you. He is light, peace, love, and freedom. You will soar as a bird in the heavenlies in the freedom and liberty of the children of God on earth, not bound by sin's chains.

I offer you life, children. True life. Let Me give Myself to you in all My fullness. I long to be united with you forever. Allow Me this gift."

God,
Jealous Father

April 6, 2018

"My life on earth was a life of bitter rejection and opposition. My intent was to save people, but My purposes were constantly misrepresented and suspected. My heart hurt Me throughout My life.

I looked at souls, realizing they were rejecting God's mercy, and My heart broke with grief. I knew what every man could become with God's mercy, yet they chose to live in sin, darkness, and fear. How few were the souls that chose to live in God's light!

I lived with the thought of My atrocious death before My eyes. I shuddered to think about the pain and agony of being crucified, yet I trusted My Father in all things. With Him, I could endure all things, even death on a cross, a cruel instrument of slow torture.

True life in Christ is the way of the cross, following Me in My sufferings. Yes, the world will oppose and reject you. You will seem to be a fanatic and an oddity, but you must persevere on your holy path, regardless of those around you who discourage you.

Finding time to sit alone with Me in your suffering will greatly ease your pain. You will begin to understand the eternal plan of suffering. Without much tribulation, you shall not enter the kingdom of God.

My remnant souls are hurt especially by those that should be an encouragement to them. That is why you should not put your trust in earthly vessels, but in God

Most Holy Who never changes. He is your Lord. "Look to Him that your face may be radiant with joy."

Your time on earth is short compared to eternity. Suffering endured during this short life span is not worthy to be compared to the eternal glory to be revealed in you.

Trust Me, My children. I see your suffering hearts. Your reward is being prepared for you in My presence. I will not let you be tempted beyond what you are able to bear.

Praise Me in these dark hours. It will ease the pain of life. Constant prayer will strengthen you.

These are days of growth in the spirit. Let God have His way with you. He has a marvelous plan for your life. Trust His leading.

Rejoice evermore. You are greatly loved."

Jesus,
God's Representative of Love

April 8, 2018

"Love and holiness combine to form saintly souls of light on earth. To love is to know God, for God is love. Men prefer darkness to light because they do not know God-love. God's love can be physically seen in everything He has so lovingly and carefully created.

To respond to God's love, you must forget yourself and ponder His heart. His loving gestures are ignored and overlooked as man focuses on His creative abilities. They forget that they are made in His image. Man craves love and so does God. Unrequited love is the grief of the soul, especially when love is betrayed by ingratitude and rebuffs.

Lift your eyes to God's heart and see His generous and lavish desire to bless His children. He looks upon each soul as His only child, so great is His concern and affection.

Even when a soul desires to become holy, many times that soul depends on activities and works trying to please God by behavior. That is all part of loving God, but His deep desire is presence, spending time together, familiar discourse, understanding His desires, truly becoming a friend of God.

To be a friend of God, you must spend time getting to know Him. You must listen to Him when He speaks. You must let Him reveal Himself to you. You must forget yourself to think of Him. You must turn away from the world and its constant distractions to keep your mind on the eternality of each moment. You must believe in His love for you and trust His judgments in your regard.

God loves a confident, joyful, trusting, abandoned, smiling child, a haven of rest in a controversial and cynical world of unbelieving adults. How His heart is refreshed when He sees a grateful, obedient, happy child of His sharing His goodness with all it encounters.

The Guardian Angel of such a soul is doubly blessed, as it has a peaceful journey to make on earth alongside its ward. Some Guardian Angels live in daily grief as they obediently walk beside a disobedient, unthankful child of God.

Your one aim in life should be to please the heart of your heavenly Father. Make Him happy with your joyful, contented smile.

So few give Him the peace to rest in their souls! There is so much agitation, doubt, and confusion. Spiritual growth is stunted in this disbelieving atmosphere.

Give God a restful place within your heart. Let Him reign in all His glory within your tabernacle of grace."

Holy Spirit,
Peace of God's Love

April 9, 2018

"The sun hides behind the clouds yet it is always shining. Just so, God hides behind a veil in your life, yet He is always there. You cannot hide from His loving gaze. He is a father to each of His children on the earth.

God has many prodigal and rebellious children. He does not execute severe judgment upon them but exercises their life in trials and tribulations to teach them eternal lessons. Those He loves, He chastises, and He prunes every tree to bear more abundant fruit.

He is severely blasphemed, rejected, and snubbed, yet He gently and patiently waits for the return of His errant ones. He wants to relieve their self-inflicted burdens but must patiently wait out the learning process.

God's wisdom uses every circumstance in a life to bring it to spiritual refreshings. Some souls climb the ladder of holiness quickly; others at a slow pace. Some souls blatantly reject all of God's advances. These are the souls most to be pitied. A hardened heart is very hard to break. Only great tragedies have converted some hardened souls.

God is loving and gentle. He does not desire the death of the sinner but rejoices in his repentance. You cannot balk against the natural laws of the universe and expect good results. Neither can you reject your Creator and hope to attain a good end.

Those who slow down in life make the most spiritual progress. They learn to meditate and contemplate the deeper meaning of life. They react accordingly. They try to place themselves in God's path, asking for His guidance.

No day is exactly the same. Each day brings unique experiences and circumstances. Like a road trip, you follow the scenery with your eyes as the car takes you to your destination.

Know that I drive the car in your life. I will take you to your final destination. If you stay in the car, obediently submitting to My will as I drive, you will arrive in heaven joyfully, having experienced a safe and happy journey. The disobedient children experience a bumpy and tumultuous ride. They do not trust the driver and constantly open the car door intending to jump out. They live in anxiety and fear because of their lack of trust in My fatherly love and care for them.

Ride to heaven with Me sweetly and safely. Sit back in the seat in quiet trust. Entertain Me by singing joyful songs of trust and abandonment. Help Me pick up stragglers on the way by your obedient will to follow Me and My leading in all things.

Our road trip will be full of love, laughter, and heavenly surprises. Your trust brightens My generosity, causing Me to bestow My abundant gifts and graces upon you.

My obedient children delight My heart!"

God,
Controller of the Universe

April 10, 2018

"Who can understand or fathom with his finite mind the love of God? Man has a lifetime to ponder God's love, but not until he has suffered for others will he begin to understand God's love. Love is completely unselfish, one's heart being given in exchange for the loved one.

God made man in His image to share His great love. Man is able to freely respond or freely reject God's creative advances. God waits patiently while man roams to and fro throughout the earth until he runs out of ideologies and activities, until he comes to the realization that he is mortal, that his life will end, and then what will matter in all he has so carefully chased after?

The more you realize you do not know, the more humble your opinion of yourself, the more childlike your openness, the more docile you are to God's opportunities – the sooner you will come to realize and understand God's great love for you. God reveals Himself to the simple, the humble, the childlike. He rejoices to commune with the pure and the innocent, the trustful and obedient souls on earth.

Thanksgiving and praise pour forth from a soul in love with God. Gratitude has a strange power over God's heart. He draws a grateful soul to Himself, showering greater and greater graces upon a thankful soul.

It is so easy to be God's friend. Open your soul to Him in sincerity. Acknowledge how little you know and ask for His nearness. He is just waiting to bless you with His fatherly presence.

God is gracious and kind, loving and gentle. He refuses no one, not even the most hardened of hearts. He sees what a soul can become if that soul is open to His grace.

I tell you over and over again to become a little child in life. The world tells you to grow up. I tell you to remain a child. The beautiful attributes of childhood – wonder, purity, innocence, lovingkindness – are the fruits that bring a heavenly fragrance to earth's barrenness.

Children do not worry or fret. They receive and go forward in joy! Their confident trust is boundless. They receive the Father's love with joy.

Become a child again. You will experience the joy of abandonment and freedom. You will walk in God's fragrant radiance upon earth. How refreshing to cynical hearts!"

Jesus,
Eternal Child of Joy

April 11, 2018

"God wants all of you – your heart, your soul, your mind, your strength, your body, your time, your activities, every breath. When you give Him all of yourself, He can do magnificent wonders. He can radiate and shine through your personage. He can speak through your words. He can think for you, reason for you, understand through you.

As you deliver yourself daily into His hands, you become an "alter Christus", another Christ in the world. The world is so in need of Jesus Christ interacting among the throngs of deadened souls. They need to come back to life by the power of the Holy Spirit. He is the breath of God that enlivens every man that enters into the world.

The Holy Spirit, the breath of God, exhales God's perfume wherever He is allowed to breathe. As you open yourselves to His holy presence within you, He exhales holiness, love, peace, joy, and all the beautiful attributes of heaven. Heaven comes to earth wherever He is embraced.

Open yourself constantly to the Holy Spirit. Let Him have his way with you. He desires to mold your life into God's pattern. He will restore all that has been marked by sin. The Holy Spirit is God's gift to souls open to His direction. An obedient and trustful heart is an open door for Him to do miraculous things on earth.

God's way of doing things is always best. Turn to Him in all your needs. He has all the answers you are seeking. Wait on Him and do not lose heart.

He will come through for you as you learn to exercise your trust. He is building a beautiful mansion in your heart brick by brick. Each brick is a virtue gained by the hard work of trust and obedience.

The way is hard, but life is short and from eternity's view, this is a drop in the ocean of eternity

Trust God and all will be well."

Holy Spirit
Strength of God's Chosen Ones On Earth

April 12, 2018

"Love enkindles a fire of love in response. Love can change any situation. As you love, you place God into any situation.

Hatred does not know how to respond to love. A loving response pours cold water on the fire of hatred's blazing wrath.

To love as God loves is to embrace suffering. Rejected love is a grief to the heart.

Insert God's love into everything in your life. The mundane will become beautiful and exciting. The boring will become meaningful and rich.

You are put on earth to learn to love as God loves. He is raising a loving family to live with Him forever.

The more you love God, the more He will draw you deeper and deeper into His heart of love. He will delicately entangle you within His heart fibers. He will send forth His glorious light into your intellect so that you may comprehend His infinite and all-embracing love.

The Blessed Virgin Mary loved God with all of her heart. Her eyes were locked into the eyes of God. She loved Him unselfishly to the point of complete self-effacement and abandonment.

Mary lived for God alone. He was never out of her thoughts. Transitory things meant nothing to her. She lived in eternity's light.

God blessed Mary with the gift of His dearly beloved Son, His treasure. He trusted her with His child. Her fidelity to grace brought her eternal veneration and praise. God truly exalts the humble.

"Draw near to God and He will draw near to you." He delights in a pure heart of love begging for His nearness.

No prayer for God's love will go unanswered. He will send the Spirit of Love into your heart immediately.

God seeks lovers, true lovers. God is love. He is the fullness of love. As you love, you become one, for He is love."

The Mystery of Love, The Holy Spirit's Call

April 13, 2018

"Purity is possible in contact with God. God, the all-pure Creator, cleanses every soul that approaches Him in sincerity and truth. To be cleansed in the Blood of Jesus is a miracle. Defilement is a leprous cancer in the world. It eats away at man's soul. It grieves his soul.

Purity was the original state of man. Sin entered, and evil concupiscence reigned in man's heart. Jesus, the All-Pure Holy Lamb of God, condescended to man's cries for mercy. He became sin for sinful man. He took upon Himself the sins of the world. He offers a cleansing bath, the cleansing blood bath, to transform and heal the sinner.

Come to Jesus, those of you marked and stained by sin. Jesus will heal you and transform your sinfulness into holiness of life. He will make your heart clean and pure. He will open the gates of heaven to you. The door is open. Will you enter?

In the prayer of repentance is your healing. In contrition and sorrow for sins is your divine transformation. The fountain is ready for you to bathe in, but so few jump into the healing waters of baptism and holy fire.

Those that come to Me I will in no wise cast out."

Jesus,
Purity

April 5, 2018

"Silence is your teacher.

Silence heals without words.

Silence convicts and converts.

Silence leads to God's holiness.

Silence is My holy and glorious language.

Nature understands My words of silence.

The heavenly bodies live in My realm of silence.

Seek silence. It will teach you about the God of the universe."

The Holy Spirit, Teacher

April 14, 2018

"My heart cry to the busy world is this: Love Me! I seek your love above all things! How few are the souls that truly love Me! Souls confess that they love Me, but they rarely spend time getting to know Me. I am not in their daily thoughts.

They run to Me in times of trouble, but in prosperity, they rarely think of Me. They talk of Me to others and say quick prayers before bedtime, but the next morning I am forgotten like mist before sunshine. They acknowledge Me as Creator, but do not know Me as Friend.

Souls live on earth as if it were their final destination. They accumulate possessions and make a name for themselves. They take excellent care of their bodies and revel in entertainment, yet I am the great Forgotten One, waiting in the background to be noticed.

To know that you have given your life for someone that disregards Your existence is very painful. Ingratitude, carelessness, lack of manners, brusque intervals of devotion, distrust, lack of meaningful conversations, utter disregard of My sacrifice – what pain this gives Me in My heart!

What more can I say to you, children of Mine? Your lukewarmness grieves Me. You have forgotten Me. You are like the nine lepers that were healed but did not return to give thanks.

My love compels Me to continually reach out to you, souls of My heart. I purchased you with My blood. I will continue to defend you before My Father. My wounds are your mercy."

Jesus,
The Forgotten One

April 15, 2018

"Snow flurries are beautiful reminders of God's unceasing graces falling upon the heads of His children. The pure whiteness of the snow whirling endlessly in circles is a sign of God's wondrous creativity.

Everything on earth is a sign of God's love. All of nature harmoniously revolves daily, submitting to the will of God in all things. The swaying of the trees in the breeze is a picture of the Holy Spirit's movement upon earth in the hearts of men. You can't see the wind, yet it moves the trees. So is the Spirit working in men's hearts moment by moment.

Only those given eyes to see comprehend each daily event as God's orchestra of praise in the world. To understand the truths of God, you must silently acquiesce to the gentle movement of the Holy Spirit within you. You must let Him lead you as a leaf on a windy day.

Jesus seeks obedient souls to move among men as He wills. Obedient trust is a joy to the heart of Jesus. He reveals Himself to the obedient children on earth.

Each soul has a unique path to glory, although some souls arrive spiritually before others because of their listening spirits. Silence is the key that unlocks many doors in the spiritual realm.

O, the glory of a silent soul! The more a soul prays, the more silent that soul becomes because the soul becomes wrapped in God, who is truly the great Silent One.

Words were given to men on earth as a gift, but they are not needed to commune with God heart to heart. They can get in the way of true intimacy with God.

Words can become a selfish way of expressing oneself. Words block the listening process. A man with a controlled tongue can become a spiritual giant.

Silence is golden. Silence teaches you eternal truths. Silence weans the soul from the world. Silence is glorious in God's eyes.

Your silent Savior waits for you to approach Him with a silent heart so that He can teach you the eternality of silence in God's presence."

The Holy Spirit, The Silent Friend

"*Every pure song of beauty has descended from heaven.*"

April 17, 2018

"Your daily fidelity to grace pleases Me. Even though you see and feel little progress, I see the eternal picture of your life.

Souls have no comprehension of eternity. If you walk the earth with the thought of eternity in your mind, everything will look different to you. You will value what is important in the light of eternity.

So sadly does man walk the earth with a closed mind to the eternal. He trudges through life as through a mud-filled field, burdened with life's pressures. He has no idea that these burdens are short-lived and fleeting.

Now is the time to walk in the steps of eternity, making every moment an eternal goldmine!

I offer you an infinite eternity, terms you cannot begin to comprehend. Through faith, you attempt to understand, but in the humility of not knowing and not understanding yet remaining faithful, is your merit before Me.

The Father seeks to lavish His love upon you eternally. He awaits your entrance through the eternal doors so eagerly. He knows your weaknesses and supplies for your needs and deficiencies. Trust His loving fatherly heart.

The journey is short in the truth of an eternal destination. Meditate on the eternality of each action and strive to glorify God in word and deed. Your works will weave a beautiful robe of righteousness that will be draped over your glorified body eternally.

See the big picture – life with God forever!"

Jesus,
Eternal King

April 18, 2018

"Animals are My gift to the world. They feed man, protect man, help man, and love man unconditionally. They are loyal and faithful, patient, and pure.

They live saintly lives on earth, for they do not sin. They are dependent. They obey their masters. They serve man on earth.

They sing songs to man from the trees. They swim the oceans, multiplying to produce food for man.

They bear burdens in the fields, carts for workers.

They provide meat and milk, leather for coverings, tusks for ornaments.

They fertilize the plants and pollinate for the food supply.

Man has been unusually cruel to these pure animals, on earth for a purpose, to sustain man.

They lock chickens up in cages because of greed. They cause dogs to fight each other. They kill animals for sport. They hang their heads on the walls of their homes to proclaim their prowess. They operate puppy mills and dog races, keeping dogs confined indefinitely. They lock parrots in cages when they yearn to fly in the open sky.

I am appalled at man's insensitivity and cruelty. Selfish greed pompously hurts the defenseless.

My world was to be a beautiful park where animals would be treated with respect, for they are so needed.

Progress has hardened man's heart. He selfishly pursues money, all the while treating the defenseless animals inhumanely.

This wounds My heart."

Jesus

April 19, 2018

"Jesus, joy of faithful souls.

Jesus, peace, light, hope, transformative love.

Jesus, friend to all.

Jesus, holy Son of God.

Jesus is the Light of the world.

Jesus-Joy is the refuge of His children. He greets them every morning with the sunshine and warmth of His everlasting love.

Jesus is the hope of the world. He destroys all despair and disappointment. He is the light in the darkness.

Jesus-Love strengthens the inner spirit to endure all things for Love's sake.

Jesus-Friend is the loving companion along the journey of life. He is always available to counsel and to guide.

Jesus-Counselor to the confused and oppressed, always comforting and urging souls to press on in holiness.

Jesus-Truth, in whom is no deceit. He leads along sure paths of righteous judgment. His paths are peace.

Jesus-Light is the lamp shining in the darkness, the hiding-place of the fearful.

Jesus-Prayer, whose words rise higher and higher on to infinity, the pleasure at God's right hand.

Jesus – all things to all men, available at any moment, ready to help, willing to forgive and instruct, compassionate to the weak, friend of sinners, counselor of the ignorant and confused.

Jesus, adoration of all saints and angels, we thank You, we adore You, we honor You, we reverence You, we praise You above all forever.

Let my mouth be filled with Your praise all day long.

You are Life.

You are Love.

You are God."

April 20, 2018

"How few are the souls receiving the gifts I promise to give to souls dedicated to the Holy Table of God, Holy Communion! Jesus is physically and spiritually present on the altar daily, hourly, there to be with souls until the consummation of the world. He tenderly awaits them, silently abiding in lonely tabernacles all over the world, where the Holy Bread is consecrated.

He waits silently, and He prays. Most blessed Jesus, ignored and forgotten in His humble abode among men, continues to annihilate Himself for the souls of God's children.

Who really understands that Jesus lives among us daily as He did in the days of the Gospel? Is anything impossible with God? Can we limit His bounteous giving of Himself?

Jesus shares Himself daily, hourly, moment by moment in the breaking of the Bread as He did at the Last Supper. He perpetuates His sacrifice upon the altar of the human heart. He longs to steal the hearts of men to turn them into glowing furnaces of love for God.

Though invisible to the naked eye, Jesus abides body, blood, soul and divinity in the consecrated Bread and Wine. Unnoticed, unappreciated, forgotten, unloved – yet He remains faithful to His cause – the will of God, returning His brothers and sisters to God's sheepfold.

Here He remains until the end of earthly time. Then He will manifest Himself in all His glory to all souls, His beloved sheep and those who have despised His gift of Himself.

Jesus, lowly servant of men, the great forgotten Shepherd of the sheep, forgive us, we pray."

Whisperings from Heaven

April 25, 2015

"Daily faithfulness to My holy will rejoices My heart. I am not looking for My children to impress Me with their works. I am seeking humble souls to be My friends forever.

To commune with a pure soul on earth is My delight, the joy of My heart. Impurity has built a wall between Me and the souls I dearly love. "The pure in heart shall see God."

As you gaze upon the simple purity of a baby, you see what I see when I gaze upon one of My pure children. I long to caress them, shelter them, protect them, and love them to My heart's content. A baby does not resist loving advances or run away from a heartfelt embrace.

Heaven is filled with purified souls that commune with God in eternal bliss. God is holy and cannot abide with sin. In the Old Testament Scriptures, all the instruments on the altar had to be purified to remain in His Presence. Even so today, much talk will not sanctify you. Only purity of heart will bless you with intimate fellowship with the Blessed Trinity.

Purity of speech, purity of the eyes, purity of intent, purity in every aspect of your life can only be attained by God's grace.

Prayer opens the doorway as you commune with God face to face. His loving countenance radiates you, clearing away your sinful desires.

A heart seeking God's will alone is on the ladder to purity of heart. A mind seeking to know and understand God's eternality begins to see a changed perspective.

Keeping oneself unstained by the world's lifestyle is a daily vigilant battle. You must never put your arms down in this fight. The world, the flesh, and the devil are the unholy trinity that try to break off your communion with God.

As you eat My Body today in Holy Communion, please meditate all day on the fact that Purity Incarnate has blessed you with His purely holy presence. Do not let your tongue utter impure things when it has entertained so great a Guest.

I am the all-pure, all-holy Jesus who loves you and longs to purify you fully in this life. Surrender all your members to Me and allow Me to wash you clean of your sins.

I am here for you, desiring to make you a pure saint in an impure environment.

"All things are possible with God."

Jesus,
Purity of God

April 26, 2018

"My loving presence surrounds you all through your day, even though you do not acknowledge or recognize My presence. Faith is not to be observed by the human eye or the senses. It is an act of the will, a gift of God, to be sure, but a determined mindset to be a disciple, a follower of Jesus Christ.

To follow the Savior, you must take up your cross daily and follow where He leads. He is the Good Shepherd, going before His flock, leading them out into the world to do the Father's bidding.

So many sheep turn back, are unruly, or run ahead of the Shepherd. How rare it is to lead peaceable and patient sheep, obediently keeping step with the Master! A weaned soul, dead to self, is docile and obedient, easily led by the Master's touch alone.

Man, in his pride, desires to do great exploits for God, but God can only use the humble soul, dead to self's ambitions, to carry out His holy will in all excellence.

It takes years to form an obedient sheep, one content to follow and not to lead. It takes many failures and falls to convince that sheep that he cannot make the journey in safety on his own.

To spend time getting to know the Shepherd gives the sheep the spiritual gift of reverence for God's great omnipotence.

Man realizes he is but dust in the presence of the all-holy God. Then, in his dust, he realizes his life-breath is a gift from his Creator. He cannot exist without his Creator's love.

God is forming a holy flock of sheep on earth. These souls are humble, docile, obedient, pure, sincere, and trustworthy. They seek no glory for themselves but only yearn for the glory of God.

These sheep traverse the hills and valleys in life perseveringly, "looking unto Jesus, the author and finisher of their faith." "In Him we live and move and have our being." They have truly found the "pearl of great price," Jesus Christ, the Redeemer of the world.

These are My gleaming jewels in the world, those "that have made a covenant with Me by sacrifice," the sacrifice of losing their lives in this world to gain it unto life eternal.

My beloved sheep, I am with you to the consummation of the world. Believe in My Shepherd's love for you. I love all of you with an infinite love. Who can truly understand the love of God?

"My sheep hear My voice and I know them." They live in My heart."

Jesus,
Shepherd for God

April 27, 2018

"Words spoken in the heart to Jesus are powerful arrows shot straight into God's heart. The cry of the soul to its Creator is a beautiful mystery in full bloom. God cherishes the simple, pure prayer of a humble soul said in earnest. He leans down from His windowsill in heaven and draws the soul upward into His glorious dwelling place.

God is like a loving mother hovering over the crib of her beloved child. He hears every sigh of your heart. Nothing passes unnoticed to His gaze. The tiniest, the littlest, the most hidden – these capture His attention immediately, for God is humble and He delights in all things humble.

Arrogance is odious to His meek and mild heart of love. He delicately lifts the humble to Himself.

Moses was the meekest man on the earth and God delighted in this holy friendship. God truly exalts the humble by allowing them into His all-embracing presence. The more you humble yourself in all circumstances, the higher God will lift you up.

Do not be afraid to appear lower in the eyes of men, for God does not see as man sees. God looks at the heart, not on the outward appearance.

To know who you are and to know who God is – this is the secret to holy humility. To know yourself, you must contemplate God. His holiness will show you your rightful place before Him.

When you recognize that you are nothing without His sustaining life-breath, then you will understand His plans for your life – a surrendered love, giving all of yourself into His wise hands. He will then have full control of your life and will be able to fulfill your holy destiny.

He created you to be a spectacle of glory in the world, radiating God's loving holiness to all souls. Only as you are transparent in His love can His light and love shine through you to others.

The highest calling is simplified and humble holiness of life. Then you will truly be a child of God, a child of the light, a chosen vessel to radiate God's light to the world."

Jesus,
Light of God's Holiness

May 5, 2018

"Your soul is drawn to Me by the living power of the Holy Spirit invading your soul. When you open yourself to Me and abandon all of yourself to Me, I come to you quickly.

My heart seeks a refuge, a haven of rest in this disenchanted and toxic world. The beauty of My creation is overlooked as man seeks ways to satiate his fleshly desires. To sit alone with Me pondering My eternal truths opens the glory of the real world to you, the eternal world of God, more beautiful than the world you see with your earthly eyes.

Truly, all is not what it seems to be. Life is a true paradox. The values of men are topsy-turvy in a broken world, a world broken by sin's invasion.

Purity of heart draws down God's graces and opens up a new vision of your reason for existence. God communicates unceasingly to the pure heart. God dwells peacefully in a pure heart.

Seek God in all things for He is all that exists. Open your heart and let Him flood your soul with His light. In innocence and purity, come before Him with gratitude on your lips and in your heart. Come with no agenda.

Let Me imprint My face upon your face. It is a matter of continual surrender to My good pleasure, seeking to please Me in all things with no thought of self.

Death to self is your highest priority. When you die to self's demands, Jesus takes over. He lives in you and can work His wonders upon earth.

So few understand the simplicity of saintliness. Become a little child, obedient to your loving Father. Love Him, obey Him, trust Him, follow His leading. Your joy will be the joy of a happy, skipping child at play, without a care in the world.

"Jesus, You answer the door." Your mother loved this phrase. I love it, too. It gives Me the privilege of taking care of all your needs without hindrance.

I wait for your loving invitation. I never barge through a closed door. Invite Me into every area of your life and live in the total surprise of the joyful, abundant living you will possess on earth.

My life on earth was suffering, but it was suffering in God's joy. There is no joy like God's joy and He willingly desires to share His eternal beatitude with His beloved children."

Jesus, God's Joy

May 7, 2018

"My Mother is greatly honored by God because of her fidelity to His love. She humbly accepted the greatest suffering known, to sacrifice her Son and her God for the sins of man. She was created by God to reveal His glory to the world, the vessel holding the Son of God within her body. Only a sanctified body could hold such an infinite treasure.

She is God's masterpiece of holiness, an icon of the grace of humble and loving obedience to God, on earth and in heaven.

Mary's maternity is a mystery known to God and His chosen saints. He reveals His passions to His friends, those that will treasure and plumb the depths of His greatest gifts.

Mary's acts remain hidden and enshrouded in a mysterious glory. God shields her from the attacks of vicious tongues. She is God's hidden jewel, softly encased in His Heart.

Mary's fragrance penetrates the souls of hardened sinners. She opens closed doors by her gentle fragrance and perfumed entrance.

Mary is sweet, gentle, and humble. She is a beautiful example of what God cherishes in a soul on earth.

She kept herself hidden away from the sinfulness of the world, abiding incessantly in God's presence through

prayer and contemplation. Her gaze was ever fixed
on God.

Mary has been given the apostolate to form holy souls
on earth through her intercessory existence at the side of
her Son in God's presence. She gently invokes God's grace
for those who entrust themselves to her motherly care.

I reveal My Mother's role in God's salvation plan to
those who are ready to receive it. God protects Mary in a
special way, keeping her hidden away from skeptics and
blasphemers.

Continue to speak to My Mother in your prayers.
She is listening and desires to assist you mightily in your
spiritual journey. She has loved you since the day of your
birth and her prayers have assisted and protected you.
Though you could not see her, she has had her eyes on
you, begging God for the graces you need to become a
saint.

Thank her for her prayers."

Jesus,
Beloved Son of Mary

May 12, 2018

"I have chosen you out of the world to be a part of My eternal family. You are already included in the family, so rest in that truth. Anguish and perplexity at your spiritual progression is a lack of faith in My declared promises to you.

Be confident that I am leading you daily. Do not concentrate on your falls and failings. They discourage you and halt your progress. With a joyful heart, look up to Me in confidence, like a happy child, knowing that I am a faithful Savior. I complete what I start.

Every soul on earth has unique struggles, unique crosses to be borne. Each cross is My gift to them to prepare them for eternity with God.

So many of My children question their crosses and chafe against them. God's ways are truly not man's ways. God fits each cross to each soul. How you carry this gift determines your progress in holiness.

Some crosses are extremely heavy. Some crosses are little and almost appear insignificant to others. Each cross carries a message from God, a message of eternal love in action.

God's closest friends have borne the heaviest crosses for love of Him. They understand the nature of sacrifice as they unite their crosses to the suffering Christ. They do not carry the cross alone. Jesus, the humble yoke bearer, walks beside them shouldering the burden, lightening the load.

Many of My children do not allow Jesus to share the cross with them. What a hard and rocky road to carry the cross without God's help! It need not be, My children. Allow Jesus into every situation you face. His gentle presence eases the pain.

Look ahead to your glorious destiny. Your life is so short in the light of eternity. You will glory in your eternal crosses when you reach the heavenly shores of eternal peace and rest.

Children, pray for perseverance in running the race set before you. Many run carrying extremely heavy burdens, but the Christ sustains them and blesses each tear-stained heart. They shall shine as stars in the heavenlies forever.

There is a reward at the end of life, My littlest ones. These sufferings are producing an eternal weight of glory laid up in heaven for you and this will be sooner than you think.

Ask Jesus to help you carry your cross this day. He is waiting to help you."

God,
Your Father of Love

May 14, 2018

"The expansion of grace in the soul coincides with the acquiring of silent interchanges with your God. God feeds your soul in the silence. He reveals Himself to open, silent hearts.

The noise of the world is crippling the saints, from the laity to the priesthood.

My people seek pleasure and entertainment. They are starving their souls which thrive on sacrifice and silence.

Only the valiantly strong can withstand the great tidal wave of evil engulfing the shores of Christianity today. It is swallowing up My people as they consume the maxims of the world and shun My laws and commands.

My elect stand alone among thousands, like the prophets in the Scripture. It was the one against the many fighting for My cause. The towers of strength of yesteryear are not found today. "Even the elect shall be deceived."

These are the days of evil foretold in Scripture, "the days of Noah." The flood is on the horizon. My people are building, planting, marrying, and are given up to pleasure. I have called them to fast and pray, not to gluttony and self-seeking pleasure.

The day of reckoning is at hand and My elect feel it in their spirit. I am moving among them calling them to prayer, self-denial, and fasting from the world.

You are not of the world. I have chosen you out of the world. You run away from Me when you run to the world and live as the world lives.

Those I have chosen that remain steadfast are few, but they are greatly blessed. This spiritual maturity is a great gift from God. They are the chosen holy souls of God standing alone in the world today, the banners of Jesus blazing from their chests.

This is My holy army, elite and alone. I am preparing them for the time of the final deluge. Souls will come streaming to them to find the Christ they have denied. They will be towers of strength in the days of Jacob's trouble.

My ways are not your ways, O holy ones of God, His chosen sons and daughters. Trust My movement among you and follow obediently where I lead. You will not understand in many circumstances, but I lead through the clouds of obscurity those I am calling to heroic acts of faith.

I lead the blind by a way they know not, but I will make the crooked places straight before them. Every valley shall be filled by their lowly obedience.

In the silence, I reveal great truths. Study My heart in the silence and you will learn the eternal wisdom of the ages, which is God's love."

The Holy Spirit of God's Truths

May 17, 2018

"In the quiet moments when you let the world go by to sit alone with Me, I heal, strengthen, refresh, and build up your soul. In My presence is fullness of joy. I speak to your heart in a language you cannot discern but which imprints My heart upon your heart.

So few souls sit alone with Me to listen to Me speak to them. They are only in tune with the world and its noise. Distractions, rapidity of pace, struggles to keep up, running here and there – this is the life of the people on earth. They have no idea that they can speak to heaven at any time to receive serenity and peace. Their souls are confused and tired, yet they do not come to Me for help.

How can you get to know Me if you do not spend time with Me? Friends spend time together. Many of My children call Me 'friend', but they have not spent any alone time with Me. They know nothing intimate about My love for them. They do not feel close to Me.

They use excuses of unworthiness to explain away their lack of effort, but they are deceiving themselves. I have beckoned to all to come to Me to be saved. The door to My heart is always open.

In the silence are hidden all the treasures of wisdom and knowledge that you need to live a godly and peaceful life on earth pleasing your Creator. God loves a peaceful, orderly life, for He is peaceful and orderly. Agitation is not of God. Confusion, fear and distress are the effects of sin.

Jesus took the sins of the world upon Himself to cure and heal the souls of men. Where are the thankful souls that live out His redemption in their daily lives?

Come to Me to be healed, My people. No one who comes to Me will be turned away. I seek all souls. I love all My children.

Speak to Me candidly and we will become friends. I will reveal My heart to you. I will bring you into My world, the world of great peace.

I am Jesus, your Savior and Redeemer. Get to know Me, for I gave My life for your love."

Jesus,
Savior-Redeemer

May 18, 2018

"Moments of glorious communion with your God, Father, and Creator are blessed by an outpouring of grace, wisdom, and mercy. Time is the treasure given to you to gather gems from heaven needed to gain heavenly rewards. To die to self means to give your time to silent encounters with your God. The flesh desires activity and entertainment. The spirit feeds on quiet rest on the heart of God in silent and peaceful waiting on Him.

Like a weaned and contented child, a mature child of God waits silently in humble expectation for God's will and God's word to be revealed in its proper time. God is never in a hurry but strides through time ordering all things to fulfill His divine purpose and plans.

You must die to your eager striving which disturbs your peace and fellowship with Me. In peace, rest on My heart and trust in My silent response of love to you. Do not let the things of life upset you. Say confidently, "It is the Lord," in every situation.

How I am pleased to look upon a quiet, peaceful, trusting child, waiting patiently for My will to be accomplished. Grasping at things shows that self is alive and kicking, ready to take control of all things. Death to self is truly death to control in every form and fashion.

All is well! Remember that! What you see with your physical eyes is deceiving. The eyes of your heart must be enlightened to see the hidden deeds of God sown in the depth of the soul.

Trust Me, My child. I have control of all things. Lack of trust wounds My tender heart. My mature children of trust gladden and warm My heart.

Will you trust Me with <u>everything</u> in your life? I am truly capable. Do you believe this, or do you doubt My goodness?

I have carried you all the days of your life. I will not fail you now as you close in on the life of the eternal kingdom awaiting you. Persevere in your tenacious desire to know Me, but let trust be your key to My peace in all areas of your life.

I am able to carry you through all the remaining moments of your short life. Trust Me in this."

Lovingly,
Jesus,
Your Friend and Caretaker

May 19, 2018

"Boundless and all-consuming love streams forth from My Father's heart. He is an ocean of love pouring forth gifts upon the earth.

Man takes everything for granted, especially God's generosity. His faithfulness keeps the world in existence.

If the sun refused to shine, all on earth would die. It is My Father's love that keeps everything alive on earth.

Man cannot run away from God's love because he is swimming in the ocean of God's existence at every moment."

August 11, 2015

"To find your Jesus within you is to live in heaven on earth. I am extraneous to so many Christians on earth. They know of me, they serve Me, they think of Me, they pray to Me, but they do not experience Me. I abide in the center of your being waiting for you to meet Me there in your spirit. You must enter the silence to find Me. I am so little known experientially because My children are too distracted, and they seek Me in noise and activity. I am the still, small voice within you that can only be really heard and understood in the silence, in those quiet moments of intimacy when you lean in spirit on My breast.

By an act of the will, you must steal away to a place of quiet to seek My presence in a very fulfilling encounter. I surround you continuously but there is a special grace of encounter that few souls recognize or understand.

The mystics ran away to live in caves and hermitages to seek the silence of our encounter. I brought Moses to the top of Mt. Sinai to talk with him face to face. I took Elijah into the desert to hear My still, small voice. John the Baptist was the voice crying in the wilderness.

The world is like a farmer's market. Men stand at their booths continually shouting out for you to taste their wares. They are noisy and garrulous, like the agitated world around you constantly calling you to forget spiritual realities.

May 20, 2018

"The trials of a just man are numerous and very rough, for I am perfecting his soul as a diamond is tumbled to show forth more glorious color and beauty.

To be left alone in your weaknesses is not a sign of God's favor. He chastens and disciplines His beloved children, for His heart is moved with pity for them.

God is bringing many sons and daughters into His glory. They must be prepared and purified. This purification comes about through trials and adversities, the best school in the spiritual life.

Immature Christians act like children when faced with a trial. They get angry like a toddler and many throw tantrums, raging at God in their grief. As a soul matures spiritually, he looks back on past experiences, realizing that trials always had a teaching tool and that God used these problems to open their spiritual eyes.

To be quiet and submissive and serene through severe trials is the mark of a truly committed follower of God, one that has been weaned from self, one that loves and trusts God, one that yearns for eternal joys and knows that all in life is fleeting and passing.

Every day will bring new situations to test your faith and endurance. Expect them. Learn to handle all things as Jesus would have while on earth. Ask Him to teach you how to respond to every circumstance.

He is molding you into an "alter Christus" by the Way of the Cross, the road He walked on earth.

God is faithful. He will help you. He will encourage you. There will be many joyful days on your journey. Your trust in His plans for you will bring a needed tranquility to your life.

Be joyful and trust God. There is no greater prescription for joy in life. It is difficult in hard times, but grace will enable you to be victorious over yourself.

"Come to Me, all ye that are burdened, and I will give you rest." To rest in God's love is heaven on earth."

Joyful Jesus

May 28, 2018

"Life is short and fleeting. Only what is done in and through God is lasting. To have eyes for the eternal is great wisdom. The god of this world has blinded the eyes of mankind. They live for the present moment, for pleasure and happy activities.

The world of God is spirit. "Those that worship God must worship Him in spirit and in truth." The truth is Jesus Christ, the Savior and Sanctifier of this world. All who speak forth the name of Jesus speak forth eternal and everlasting truth.

All who run to Jesus for refuge shall be protected from the deception of the Evil One. He controls the world's powers, the media, and the laws of men. He rules his invisible kingdom with a ruthless and raging hand. He seeks to destroy, to ruin, to kill, and to maim all men on earth. He uses subtleties of beauty to mask his façade of goodness. He entraps souls, alluring them with the pleasures of the senses.

Once they are addicted and entrapped, he abandons them in their weakness, searching for new victims to destroy. He especially seeks to destroy reputations and to discourage the hopeless and faint-hearted. He alienates and isolates, cherishing secrecy and hidden deeds of darkness.

Satan seeks especially to destroy Christians. He tries to steal their prayer times, humiliates them through people, discourages them in trials, and seeks to keep them oppressed and failing. He wants to shield their minds from the truths of Christ's power within them.

He causes fighting, division, and broken relationships. He rejoices to see the fall of a city, a generation corrupted, a political regime that is atheistic and controlling, and the variety of heretical cults that enslave its members.

These sheep are herded into prison pens unknowingly. They follow Satan blindly into these dens of darkness, never thinking to call out to the God of light for deliverance.

Their delusions of grandeur imprison them into a false sense of security as the days go by bereft of any treasure accumulation in heaven.

So it is on earth with mankind. I stand at the crossroads pointing out the eternal road to salvation, but the blinded sheep obediently follow their master, Satan, to their doom. "Narrow is the road that leads to life, and few there be that find it."

Be vigilant, My people, for Satan seeks to devour and destroy you. He seeks your slip of the tongue, your hidden sin, your choice of friends, your daily habits, to allure you onto his road of dark deeds.

Resist him in the powerful and holy name of Jesus. Cry out to God in repentance and He will rescue you. He will deliver you from the mouth of the lion.

Your best defense against Satan's schemes is to spend time in My presence. There I will stamp you with

My image of strength and beauty. There I grant you My wisdom and My grace to understand the wiles of the devil.

My little ones, the time is short. Stand on guard in prayer and watchings. The hireling is stealing the sheep in droves and there are no shepherds to rescue them. Each has gone to his own house of pleasure.

Will you be a holy sheepherder in My name, rescuing those caught in the jaws of death? You will save a soul from death and cover a multitude of sins.

My invitation is before you. Will you join Me in My rescue efforts?"

Jesus,
Sheepherder

July 27, 2018

"The glorious and holy souls of the just abide in the heavenly corridors, praising and blessing God continuously. The air of heaven sparkles with a holy glow of peace. Heaven is a continual festival of love.

God abides among His holy children in great delight. His sons and daughters are His joy. They are made in His image and He rejoices over them. His heart is full as He looks upon their faces of light and love, adoring Him in spirit and truth.

This land of fountains and rainbows is the country of eternal bliss and beatitude. There is no pain, crying, or misunderstanding. All is well in the City of Light forever and ever. The angels marvel at the mercy of God resting upon His beloved ones. God will ever be their God and Father throughout the endless ages of eternity, world without end. They will forever be singing His praises.

The door is open to this City of Light, but only the pure and holy are allowed to enter. Those purified and cleansed by the Holy Blood of Jesus are welcomed and loved with God's everlasting love.

This is God's wonderful and magnificent handiwork, the crux of His creation – to live forever in His presence, transformed into His image, children of God eternally.

This is the glorious inheritance of the saints in light."

Holy Murmurs from Heaven

May 29, 2018

"Frustrating days on earth will come often. This is the lot of being a human. Your flesh wars against your spirit incessantly. It is a continual warfare. You must not lay down your arms in discouragement, but go forth boldly in My name, relying on My strength within you.

Do you not yet believe that all in your life is part of My divine plan for you? Can you trust that I lead you daily, that I inspire you to repent when you fall, that I use the little daily occurrences to accomplish My will in you?

Things are not what they seem to you. I see things on earth with a completely different perspective. I watch to see how you handle daily conflicts and pressures, how you treat other people, how you rise after a fall, how you handle frustrating circumstances, how you listen for My instructions. Your efforts to do better bring joy to My heart.

You are living in a dark world that has forgotten God. You must know that this is a difficult course. Very few souls encourage you in your heart's desire to live a holy life. You stand alone in a world closed off to the spiritual dimension. It is difficult to walk bravely forward with no spiritual feedback from daily encounters. I see your efforts to remain faithful to Me daily.

You know you are hard on yourself and you know that I know your deepest intentions. Deep in your soul you know that I am not disappointed with you.

You have been given some heavy crosses to bear emotionally since childhood. I understand your feelings of unworthiness and shame. These crosses keep you from being arrogant or proud. They keep you in a humble frame of mind, always thinking others better than yourself. That is not a bad thing.

This rainy and dark day will pass quickly. Do not turn back in discouragement now. You have come so far in your journey to your homeland.

Keep coming to Me in your pain and struggles. We will work things out together.

I always have your eternal best interests at heart."

Jesus,
Brother

May 30, 2018

"Behold My body stripped and hanging, forlorn, nailed to wood. This I allowed for love of you. I have shown My love to the world by this horrendous sacrifice of My life.

My sacrificial love is ignored. I am left alone in My pain and agony to suffer for the sins of the world. I humbled Myself for My Father's good pleasure, to bring many sons to glory, to rescue those in captivity, enslaved to their passions and the lusts of the world.

My cross is blood-stained with My love. It is raised high over the world, the remedy for all evils. In My vulnerability, I let Myself be trampled on by humanity. Even today, the trampling continues. My name is blasphemed, My followers in lukewarmness betray Me, My shepherds lord it over the flock.

Through the storm of evil, I am forming saints of love to join Me in eternal praise of My Father. The souls walk a lonely path of obscure faith, keeping their eyes on Me through all circumstances. Each soul carries a cross, hand-cut and carved uniquely for each child of God.

The life of a saint is not easy. It is a heroic life, for the visible rewards are few and far between. Faith promises them an eternal reward if they persevere on the journey.

It is very easy to veer off the path of sanctity, for temptations assail souls all through life, yet those who look to God in His strength and put no confidence in themselves become lions in the face of danger.

I call My souls to the high roads of sanctity, but so few are able to die to themselves and their ambitious aspirations. They have not been weaned from their lively passions. They have not truly abandoned themselves to Me.

Those that give Me all of themselves shall persevere and I will grant them the gift of holiness, the Holy Spirit living triumphant in them. Though they fall, they shall rise quickly in My strength and I will bless them with My presence all the days of their short lives."

Jesus,
Just Friend

May 31, 2018

"You are living in the final age of grace. Soon the curtain will fall, and the days of Antichrist will begin.

The battle foray has become wearisome and bitter. Many Christians have fallen by the wayside in despair. They have taken off My holy armor of prayer and sacrifice. The journey was too hard for them, so they turned back in the day of battle.

To stay strong in these evil days requires that you spend much time in God's presence, saturating yourself in His Spirit.

There is no support in the world for a life of holiness, only constant opposition. The pace of life gives a soul no breathing time, no solitude, no time to meditate on the eternality of life. Most souls are caught up in the whirlwind of nonstop activity. They are worn out and burnt out. Spirituality seems burdensome. There is no time to feed the soul.

I understand the difficulties to aspire to union with God in this hyperactive and difficult period of time. Heroic souls keep the focus on Jesus, regardless of the cost. They determine to make Him the center of their existence on earth. They have fallen in love with Him. They cannot do otherwise than to love and serve Jesus.

I have consistently told you that the road to God's kingdom is narrow, and very few find it.

God is merciful, but only the pure in heart and fervent in spirit will enter His circle of intimacy with the Blessed Trinity.

What a blessed invitation spurned on earth! Only on the day of judgment will the recognition of what a man has truly lost will be apparent to his grieved soul.

"Men loved darkness rather than light, because their deeds were evil." Men shun the light of God to pursue darkness, the world's empty way of thinking and living.

The wise will shine as the sun in My Father's kingdom of light. Though they suffered on earth, they shall rejoice eternally in God's loving embrace."

Jesus,
Sun of Righteousness

June 1, 2018

"The world is furiously angry. There is no self-restraint. Self rules in all its glory. When fleshly appetites rule, man becomes degraded and brutish, putting even the animals to shame.

It is a hard thing to contend with a hardened and angry soul. Pride has narrowed the heart. Only sin satisfies at this point. All self-restraint is cast away ... each man for himself.

In My Scriptures, I foretold the truth of this question: When I return, will there be any faith in the world? I know how evil the heart can be when it rejects God and His laws. There is no remedy but repentance, but man refuses to humble himself before Me in repentance.

This is a grievous time on earth. The souls of the just are sorrowful and amazed at the baseness of man's ideals. Hatred has replaced love. Convenience has replaced self-surrendering sacrifice.

The churches are empty. The bars are filled with happy revelers. My holy day, Sunday, has become a day for sporting events and parties. God is not in all their thoughts.

What a world you live in! It is dark and dangerous. You must continue to allow Me to fill you with My light and love to be able to persevere courageously in these final days of battle for souls. I have My special lights in the world, streaming out pathways for the stragglers to find, but they truly are few and far between.

My faithful little ones, stay close to Me. Allow Me to penetrate you with My light. Souls need to see light-bearers in the darkness.

You will walk alone on your path, but you are not alone – I am with you. I will never leave you or forsake you. You are My child of the light! In My presence, your light will be enkindled and will flare up gloriously, opening the skies of heaven to earth.

God is faithful. Arm yourselves with courage, trust, and hope.

All is well. Your God is leading you."

Jesus,
Trail Blazer for God's Holiness

"Sanctity is being in love with God."

June 2, 2018

"My grace is the sunshine in your love that causes you to radiate My Essence to souls in your environment. Though all of these signs are invisible to the eye, My penetrating presence is changing hearts and lives. It is in the silent hiddenness that I do My greatest works.

Man proclaims his prodigies, but in My humility, I work in secret, letting the fruits manifest themselves quietly and unobtrusively. Only years later do souls gratefully acknowledge and thank Me for My great gifts of grace, mercy, and love. I am willingly patient to allow them to find their way to Me after years of futile struggles. I am behind the veil, encouraging, uplifting, sustaining, and defending them, though I am rarely acknowledged.

I am the eternal loving parent, seeking the highest and best for My children. I do not want to demand that they love and serve Me. I want them to willingly fall in love with Me because of My sacrificial gentle compassion and love for them.

My love is a divine love, incomprehensible to frail and weak mankind. My love drove Me to come to earth to sacrifice all that I am for the sons of men. I seek their reciprocal love with innocent purity of intention and sincerity.

It is so easy to please Me. Just love Me in purity of heart. I know you are too weak to do more than you are capable. I will do the rest.

Let Me make you into what I have conceived for you from all eternity. Let My glory rays transform you into an angelic being on earth.

Souls need to see the angels. Angelic visitations increase faith on earth. I desire My saints to live as angels on earth – pure, innocent, loving, always doing good, glorifying God constantly.

Lie still beneath My gaze of love. This will allow Me to transform you into a radiant angel of light upon the earth. Your presence will lead souls to Me without words.

Those who seek Me <u>always</u> find Me."

Jesus,
Lover from on High

June 4, 2018

"Jesus abides in the quiet spaces of life, the hidden corners of your mind, the silent whispers in your heart. He is gentle and meek, never pushy or coercive. He is love and love endures all things with equanimity.

To know Jesus, you must be quiet and still. Noise drowns out His wise instructions. He abides in the stillness, the peace of quiet meditation, in the silent language of the eternal, where there is no time or limit.

Your realm is visual, noisy, tactile, and earthy. My realm is invisible, silent, ethereal, and heavenly.

My world is like the mist that settles over a quiet city at dawn. Your world is like the rush hour traffic, bustling with activity.

Saintly souls flee from the noise of the world, for it has silenced God in their hearts. They seek the silence, to listen ever more closely to the voice of their Beloved.

Time waits for no man. The sands in the hourglass drop one by one and the moments slip by, never to be recaptured. Lives spent in frivolous activity can never be relived, only grieved.

There is a day of judgment for every living soul to account for time spent on earth. Who did you serve? will be asked of you, and you have to answer – self or God. Will you know your Creator? Will you recognize His voice?

Now is the day of salvation. My Spirit constantly is speaking to your spirit, but can you hear Him above the noise? If you listen intently, the silence will speak to you and you will hear God.

God's voice will change your heart, your ideas, your plans, and your mindset. You will know that you do not know, that you must seek truth from the Source – Jesus Christ, God's only Son. He will lead you to the Father. The Holy Spirit will breathe upon you and divinize your life, making you a glory icon of God's grace, existing for the praise of God's glory.

I speak to those who will stop to listen. I instruct and guide My followers, keeping them on the path God has destined for them from all eternity.

Who is listening? My blessing falls upon all the listening ears and hearts on earth."

Jesus,
Speaker for Heaven

June 5, 2018

"My true light is hidden in the lowly, humble, and hidden souls that seek My glory for love of Me. They seek not great things for themselves, but faithfully serve Me in their daily duties, in many difficult circumstances. They have truly forfeited their lives in this world to claim it eternally with God.

God abides among the humble on earth. Where there is humility, you will find God.

Instead of striving to be known and admired, strive to be unknown and hidden. That is the silent path of Jesus, glorifying God by His hidden life on earth.

For thirty-three years, the God and Creator of the world lived humbly in the unknown and rarely visited town of Nazareth.

He faithfully was subject to Joseph and Mary, worked quietly at his trade, and attended the synagogue faithfully, living a hidden life of prayer, the constant communion of His soul with His Father in heaven. He sought no acclaim or praise and hid His gifts from others.

His holy Mother kept to herself, the model of sanctity on earth. St. Joseph, a humble and just man, always obediently followed the will of God where it led.

This holy family is the perfect model of family faith on earth and the simplicity of humble living, which is so pleasing to God.

St. John the Baptist declared, "He must increase. I must decrease." These words were spoken under the inspiration of the Holy Spirit who declares all the mysteries of God. My people would do well to reexamine this exhortation to humility of life.

The world grasps after fame, power, recognition, and stardom. This is great pride in action. God truly resists the proud but gives grace to the humble.

The lower you descend on earth, the greater your status in heaven, and the nearer God draws to you. He is humble and loves the humble and pure in heart.

My children, put these words into practice and your life will change. This is sanctification in action."

Holy Spirit, Sanctifier

June 6, 2018

"Love is My Holy Spirit reigning in the world. The loving gift of creation was the handiwork of My Holy Spirit of love.

The Holy Spirit is the sign of God's humility. He creates all things but remains in the background, hidden, silent, and humble. He hovers over all of creation restoring, sustaining, breathing God's life into all that exists.

He is the ocean that you swim in daily, the atmosphere of your existence. He animates you and gives you creative thought. He distills as the dew from heaven, leaving radiant and glistening dewdrops of grace on men and animals and plant life at every second of the day.

He is a mist of God, daily watering the earth. He is the water of life, refreshing the earth, cleansing, and soaking the ground to make it fertile.

The Holy Spirit lives contentedly in the souls of My children. Those that rest in His love are His special delight. He permeates their being with life, light, and love. He draws them into the Father's embrace.

The Holy Spirit is God's love in action on earth. He whirls about the earth like the endless clouds in the sky sheltering, bringing the beautiful breezes, and watering the earth with God's graces.

My children, recognize the presence of the loving Holy Spirit who sanctifies you and leads you to intimacy with the circle of Our love.

If you will allow it, He will carry you away from the dregs of earth and cause you to live in the high places upon earth, the place where earthly cares do not touch or trouble you. His divine power will rescue you from evil and temptation and He will give you the strength of a God to resist evil.

Invoke His aid. Become intimate with Him. Call upon Him incessantly. Get to know Him. Remember His loving mercy toward you.

He will help you in every circumstance. He will fill you with His love, peace, and joy, which will change your life on earth from mundane drudgery to heavenly and glorious living.

These truths need to be lived out. Ask for His help.

He is the author of your sanctification."

Jesus,
Full of the Holy Spirit

June 7, 2018

"When your heart is failing and despair sets in, come to Me, regardless of your desires.

Emotions are troublesome and fragile. Your <u>will</u> must control your emotions. You are the captain of the ship of your body and at times your emotions will be in mutiny against what your spirit knows you should do.

The best defense against veering from the path of God is to set your will before God, allowing Him to direct you daily. Do not listen to the voices within you that try to discourage you and cause you to step backwards.

Life is a daily test – to serve God or to serve yourself. To serve God requires perseverance and discipline. To serve yourself is pleasing and more relaxing. Pleasure has a louder voice than temperance and doing the right thing, regardless of how you are feeling. You must learn to distinguish your emotions from your will to serve God.

When you have failed the test, quickly repent, and then get back again on the holy highway of God's chosen ones. If you take your eyes off God, even for a moment, life takes on a completely different hue.

God's ways are not the ways of man. What looks ridiculous in the eyes of man is many times very noble in the eyes of God. To sacrifice an active life for a monastic life looks like a scandal to the world, but not in the eyes of the heavenly court.

Keep your gaze fixed on Me constantly. You will fall easily if you lower your gaze. You are walking through minefields on earth, a war zone, and the lanes are littered with dead bodies, those that have abandoned all things spiritual.

Without the light of Christ, souls, although walking, are dead. There is no life in them, for I am Life. Without Me, they are corpses in the world.

Curbing your conversation during these emotionally turbulent times would be very wise for you. You regret spoken outbursts so frequently.

Trust that I have all things under control. I see all; I know all. In My time and according to My plan, you will be released from this burden."

Jesus,
Loving Guide to Heaven

June 8, 2018

"Not all souls are granted to feel the depths of the love of My Sacred Heart.

To many souls I am a Creator-God existing in the heavenlies, far removed from their daily lives.

Many souls see Me as a hard taskmaster ready to pounce upon them in any error.

Some souls like the thought of Me, but never come to know Me intimately.

Some souls are afraid of Me. They call it humility, but many times it is the false humility of not truly making an effort.

Some souls are too busy for Me and only seek Me in tragic circumstances. The churches fill up in world tragedies.

Some souls are disappointed with Me because I didn't answer a specific prayer.

Some souls think I am all rules and regulations, always striving to take away their freedom and keep them in bondage.

Some souls do not believe that I could be interested in their little world, which is a lack of faith in My promises spoken in Scripture.

Some souls choose to live in spiritual ignorance, because the world is too exciting and alluring.

There are very few souls that befriend Me, that spend time getting to know Me, that lose their life in this world to live according to My desires.

These souls are so rare, and many times hidden from men's eyes. Their prayers are extremely powerful with God because they ask according to His will. The Holy Spirit prays within them.

These souls are rarely rewarded in life. They await eternal glory. Like St John the Baptist, their life breath is – "He must increase, and I must decrease."

These gentle souls of Mine are powerhouses on earth, though they do not know it. They generate light and life to souls by their existence. They bring heaven to earth. Their fragrance is subtle, but intoxicating. They change the atmosphere around them. They emanate God's graces through their bodily presence.

"The meek shall inherit the earth." My meek, lowly, and gentle friends walk the earth with Me. We cry out to God for the souls of men. We adore the Father in spirit and in truth.

My cross bearers walk behind Me joyfully singing My praises. They will enter the heavenly city rejoicing.

These are My best friends for all eternity."

Jesus,
Friend Seeker

June 12, 2018

"The light of the world is Jesus.

The light in My saints is decreasing instead of blazing out into holy fires. Distractions, worldly pleasures, no time for prayer, no holy goals – these are stealing the light from My chosen ones.

The world's sin increases daily. As the light dims, the darkness takes control and reigns without hindrance.

I have commanded My saints to be lights in the world, to let their light shine before men to glorify My holiness. My disobedient children have neglected and ignored the Savior of their souls. How wounded and grieved I am that I am so easily forgotten, and even worse, offended daily by their sins of negligence and dishonor!

The graces of the Holy Spirit are poured out upon My children of the light, yet He is stifled and hindered by self-will and a lack of love for Me.

The quiet and humble souls are few. The active and loud souls are the norm.

The inner man must be strengthened, the self-will must be weaned against prideful noise.

My silence is not heard. There is too much noise. Noise of talk, noise of thought, noise of activity, noise of endless entertainment.

I foretold that men would turn away their ears from hearing truth to believe in cunningly devised fables.

Today is as it was foretold: "Even the elect shall be deceived."

Prayer and sacrifice wins souls. As My prayerful souls beg for grace and mercy, I send forth My light and My truth.

Mercy will triumph in My time.

Children, seek the silence. There you will find Me."

Jesus,
The Silent Lover

June 13, 2018

"My entrance into your heart commences with your 'yes', your willingness to allow Me to become everything to you. When all the doors and windows of your being are opened to My Holy Spirit, He invades and permeates you with His holy presence. Springs of living water trickle from your inner being which develop into fountains of gushing living water that pour forth abundant riches and blessings upon the parched earth, the dry and lifeless souls of men.

Your part is to lie still beneath His holy touch. Your submission and docility give Him full access to you. He can work marvelous graces in a quiet and prayerful soul that has forsaken the world to be set apart for God's glory.

To advance in the spiritual life is a sign of God's great love for you. He has poured forth His grace and mercy upon your soul. He has opened your spiritual eyes to discover His realm.

What a stupendous gift to come to know and understand the mind and heart of God Almighty! He opens Himself to all, but so few are interested in really getting to know Him. It takes the effort of leaving the world's ways to enter His paths which are obscure, especially in the beginning of your spiritual journey. As you follow the rugged terrain before you, He teaches and instructs you in His ways, which are diametrically opposed to the world's ways.

To be set apart by God is a wondrous grace. To be called into His service is the highest honor. To be His intimate friend is beyond any imaginings on earth.

Seek nothing but God alone and He will change your heart from fleshly to spiritual. You will see life through different eyes, God's eyes.

God alone is your heart cry."

Jesus,
God Lover

June 14, 2018

"Words are extremely powerful. Words create and destroy. I came as the <u>Word</u> of God in human flesh. By your words you will be saved or condemned.

I came to set captives free. My death on the cross was more than sufficient to release souls from fleshly bondage. Use My powerful name to pronounce and proclaim My will, for I have already triumphed over sin in the heavenlies and on earth.

My name is powerful. My name pulls down strongholds and destroys fortresses. The demons tremble when they hear My name proclaimed with powerful authority.

I told My apostles: "You will do greater works than I do on earth." I gave them the power to speak forth truth and release from bondage through My powerful name.

My children do not recognize or understand the authority I have conferred upon them. I live within them. It is I doing the works within them. When My children speak forth in My name, I rise to the occasion.

A confident son or daughter of God enrages the netherworld. They are powerless before My name. They tremble under My authority.

Lukewarmness, mediocrity, and spiritual stalemate make My children completely powerless in the face of evil. As My children grow strong in My strength, fortresses crumble and are destroyed.

St. Paul said: "I can do all things through Christ which strengthens me."

You, My children, have the same power to do all things in My name. Do you believe this? If you do, and if you act upon these truths, you will see great wonders in your world.

I said: "When I return, will I find faith on the earth?" So many of My children are weak and helpless when they should be opening prison doors and setting captives free.

You must go forth in the power of the Holy Spirit to set souls free in My name. You must be holy and sanctified to have the power to sanctify others.

Open your heart wider to receive all I desire to give you – My strength, My power, My sanctity, My prayer life, My adoration of our Father.

Go forth today in your dignity as a child of God. You have all power and authority over the enemy in My name.

Be confident as David before Goliath. I will fight for you. You have only to declare a thing, and I will see that it is accomplished according to the will of My holy Father."

Jesus,
Prayer Warrior in Heaven and on Earth

June 17, 2018

"Each soul has a unique journey to live out on earth. I am the Master Gardener and I tend each plant in a different way. All must redound to the glory of God. I bring forth beauty in each and every plant, but in different ways.

Each plant must bloom in the environment that I have planted it in. Each plant must lift its petals to the sun each day to be nourished. It must drink in the living waters of My Holy Spirit within it.

Each plant is a part of a glorious landscape design arranged to please the eyes of My holy Father.

In quietness and peace, you must allow Me to direct your activities daily. I prune and tend your vines in order to keep you fragrant, lush, and beautiful in the garden of saints.

My weaned flowers are My greatest delights. They allow Me to do with them what I desire, never resisting My actions around them or in them.

A spiritually mature plant in My holy garden on earth is a glorious diadem in tribute to the great Creator God.

So you can see that humble patience and obedience keep you in the will of God, a plant tended to by God. Allowing Me to control your life brings fresh growth spurts and beautiful arrays of glorious blooms.

There is a season of growth in every soul. There is also a dormant season. You must be patient and attentive through the dormant seasons of your life.

Let My aspirations be your aspirations. Have no goal but to lie still beneath My guiding hand, the hand of a Master Gardener.

I am preparing a beautiful bouquet for My Father. The beauty and the fragrance will bring earth's perfume to heaven. My saints are My wreath of glory around My head.

Who can understand My love and mercy? Only a fellow gardener, those that seek out the flowers among the thorns of earth.

I make all things beautiful in My time."

Jesus,
Gardener from Heaven

June 19, 2018

"Little ones seek everything from their God. They know they are little and weak, and God helps them. You are made out of dust formed into clay. What can clay do? When I breathed My Spirit into your lifeless clay body, I gave you a soul. You were My creation, formed and developed in My mind from all eternity.

Everything in the world is My creation. This is the reason that creatures should obey their God. They are formed creatures. I am the God that created them.

I only ask for love and obedience from My souls clad in dust. This world is My masterpiece. I run the universe. Souls in rebellion do not destroy My master plan. They cut themselves off from My life and light. They harm themselves. It wounds My heart to see them reject all I have created for them. I am a loving parent raising many unruly children.

My little ones, I seek your love. Your works add nothing to My greatness. "By Me all things consist." I animate your hands to do the works.

I live in the world of spirit. Your fleshly works pour forth from your spiritual mindset. When you love Me, all you do becomes holy in My sight, no matter how insignificant. Love divinizes all your yearnings for Me.

This world of spirit is hidden and secret. Only those that seek Me with all their hearts find the secret door to the spirit world.

Walk through the door of spirit today. I will show you the beautiful kingdom of God hidden away from the world, waiting to be found by men with pure hearts."

Holy Spirit of the Kingdom

June 22, 2018

"Do you yet realize how much I love you, My children? You are like delicate little eggshells, fragile in your emotions, sensitive and caring about others. You bewail your faults immediately and keep running to Me for cleansing and help.

I know your frailties and your weaknesses. Continue to confess your faults and failings before My holy throne of grace. I acknowledge your admission of sin and guilt and I lovingly, eagerly, and willingly forgive you.

Though you fall a hundred times in an hour, keep running into My arms of love. I am your refuge. These sins will not hinder your journey to heaven if you confess them readily and seek to amend your ways.

All men on earth are sinners, born into sinful flesh. It is your duty while living to conquer yourselves, to abandon yourselves to your Creator who is shaping and forming you into a citizen fit for heaven.

Discipline and chastisements conform souls to My will. Sainthood is your goal for living.

Men pursue earthly goals of no consequence. Their days pass in futile undertakings of no eternal value. Their works will be burned up on the day of judgment when they will stand before Me naked of soul.

My children, the sheep in My flock, have acclimated themselves to My lifestyle of purity and holiness. They eagerly desire to enter My kingdom washed, cleansed, and purified in My blood.

They follow <u>Me</u> on earth, not the world.

You are on the right path. Seek My face and you will live the abundant life I have promised you.

Come to Me daily to be renewed and refreshed in My cleansing blood."

Jesus,
Savior

June 23, 2018

"The natural fruits and vegetables of the earth have healing powers hidden within them. The leaves of the various trees hide cures for many illnesses of your epoch.

The earth holds many secrets for mankind to discover. The bark of the trees holds many properties of healing. The moss in the forest is valuable for new scientific discoveries. All things on your planet have a secret that only a certain key can unlock.

Many scientific discoveries were made by men of meditation and prayer. They sought answers in the spiritual realm, for God knows all. If the scientists of earth would seek My face, I would teach them many things.

"Ask and ye shall receive. Seek and ye shall find. Knock and the door shall be opened unto you." All who ask receive from My hand treasures of wisdom and knowledge.

Just as your hand moves across the page while writing these words, My answers come to souls in the daily activities of life.

To seek the eternal realm is to seek to know the mind of God, who has the keys to unlock every treasure hidden in the earth.

You ask Me what is the cure for cancer and I will tell you. Sin is an infection that fights against the human race. It is inherent in the cells of a man when he is born. As you are exposed to the cursed elements in the world, cursed by the effects of man's sinful condition, your body breaks down and cells mutate.

Death is the lot of every man. Bodies degenerate and die. It is the lot of the human condition.

Cancer is the curse of the human morphology of the cell cycle. Can it be reversed? Yes, by regenerating new life into the cell.

How can that be done? What generates life? The breath of God.

Oxygen is life-producing. How can oxygen regenerate a cell? Through infusion.

Chlorophyll is your answer. Green plants heal diseases. Life-giving chlorophyll brings life to deadened cells.

"The leaves of the trees are for the healing of the nations."

Jesus,
Secret Sharer to Humble Souls

June 25, 2018

"Magnificent gestures of love in the humble whispers of prayer from the heart...

I am found in the solitude and quiet of the hidden prayer closets in the world. In prayer, you come to know who you are in Christ before God. Your place in God's family is shown to you.

My elect know My voice. They understand My yearning love for them. Their desires are to please Me in all that they do. They are My beloved children of love on earth, fulfilling My will heartily and joyfully.

My graces and blessings surround their steps. I lead and guide them daily to grow in grace and love. Our relationship is eternal in the heavens. They shall rule and reign with Me as My beloved and honorable children eternally.

Such are the littlest ones, the children on earth that seek My glory alone. I shall clothe them in white garments of light, transparent in beauty, glowing with My light in the heavens.

O children, examine your destiny! It is glorious, ethereal as the light, and noble. Walk in the strength and power of the Holy Spirit as a dignified child of God.

You are not defeated. You are more than conquerors through Christ Jesus, the King of Kings and Lord of

Lords. He is the conquering King of the ages, and you carry His banner.

Carry it high through your life, for your eternal future is unspeakably glorious."

Jesus,
Star of Heaven

June 26, 2018

"Open your soul to My light. It streams from heaven into an open and waiting vessel. Earth needs heaven's rays of holiness. It sits in darkness. I need channels of grace and mercy to pierce the dark land.

There is no hope in men's hearts. They have strayed so far from Me that they cannot find their way back. They need the light of life to illumine the path for them.

My children of light are hiding their light from the world. Sinful habits, lack of prayer, lukewarmness, earthly pleasures – they have dimmed the light of My saints. They have left My banquet table to feed on the swine husks of the world – pleasure, entertainment, trifles to waste time.

The sands of time left in the hourglass are few. God's days of judgment are on the horizon. The men of earth will face great fear and confusion. They will not know where to turn except to those who carry the light of God.

It truly is a struggle to be a light-bearer among souls in the darkness. It is easier to give up and join them in their pleasantries. But you must stand strong for them in My strength. They will need you in the coming days of crises.

The world's system is spinning out of control. There is no peace – only distress and anxiety. There is no solitude or meditative contemplation in nature. There is no inner love radiating out to others. Selfishness reigns supreme.

I have warned souls through My prophets through the centuries. How few have responded to My warnings! How the children have suffered through all of this!

Keep your gaze locked in My gaze. That is the only way you will survive the onslaught of the evil coming upon the world at the end of the age.

All has been predicted in My Scriptures. It shall come to pass.

Blessed is he that heeds the warnings of God."

Holy Spirit of Truth

June 27, 2018

"The body gets old and decays. It hastens to its first beginnings – the dust of the ground. The body is only the casement for the eternal soul, to be used for a time and then discarded.

Take care of your outer shell but do not place too much importance on its longevity. Many souls die young, regardless of their painstaking effort to sustain their body's faculties.

Advertising and the media focus solely on the body. The soul is completely ignored. How backwards the world's ways are, giving importance to things that are useless and ignoring the eternal soul, a treasure beyond compare!

You must feed and nourish your soul daily with My life and My light. You cause your flesh to rejoice when your soul is well-fed on Jesus Himself. He is your nourishment on earth, your daily Bread from heaven.

Jesus handfeeds His chosen ones with revelations of His glory. There are no words to describe what they receive on earth.

The friends of Jesus live a life of heaven on earth. They converse with Jesus daily as friend to Friend. They feel His heartbeat within them. They sense His wounded heart and His overpowering love and mercy.

Jesus, rejected by the world, but dearly loved by His friends on earth. They have turned their backs on the world and run after Jesus in all things.

They crave intimacy with Jesus above all earthly desires. Their bodies are secondary, their desires fall by the wayside, their ambitions are only to seek the beautiful face of their greatest love, Jesus.

Such are the faithful friends of God, a peculiar people to the world, but dearly beloved by God.

My little children, I see your little tokens of love toward Me and I cherish them. You are so dear to My heart. We will meet soon, and all your dreams will be realized beyond your greatest expectations."

Jesus,
Rewarder of His Holy Friends

June 28, 2018

"The health of a nation corresponds to its spiritual measure and tone. Like music, if something is out of key, the entire song sounds disharmonious.

This nation has been in open rebellion against My laws for many years now. There have been many souls true to the faith, but they have been hidden away from the world.

Satan has taken this nation captive without much intervention on the part of zealous souls. But I have heard the prayers of My oppressed people, their hands tied by the evil of technology and the media.

Parents have struggled to raise godly children, facing horrendous obstacles. I have heard their prayers. I have seen their tears. My heart is moved with pity for them.

Never in the history of the world has sin been so highly esteemed and lived out. America's sin rises as a stench in the nostrils of a holy God, and they are deporting their sinfulness to all the places in the world, through the media and the internet.

As Korah was thrown into a sinkhole when he rebelled, a sinkhole is opening in the country to swallow the sinful, rebellious souls. What has been hidden will be brought out into the light of day for all to see. I will vindicate My chosen souls that pray day and night for this country.

My hand is upon your leader. He walks with purpose in My strength. He could not continue this battle on his own.

He has been brought forth for such a time as this, to make My intents known to a sinful and rebellious nation. I do not always choose the most logical person to show forth My glory. I have surprised many nations and people with My choices in leaders.

Stand back and watch. See what I am doing. I am doing a new thing on earth. I am fighting My battles with a warrior king, equipped from birth for this position of authority. Many will fall before him and the thoughts of many hearts will be revealed. What has been hidden will be brought into the light.

I am a God of consequences. The unrighteous shall not rule forever. I intervene to straighten what has been crooked.

Watch Me work.

Watch and pray."

God,
Warrior for Righteousness

July 9, 2018

"Time stands still for no man. Fill each moment with God. God is love, peace, joy, rest, contentment. As you seek His face, you become a God-vessel on earth, shining forth His attributes to souls blinded by darkness.

My light reaches into your inner being, illuminating and cleansing, healing and restoring, making you into an "oak of righteousness," able to stand strong in Me in the fierce tempests coming upon the earth.

I am building a spiritual edifice within you, brick by brick. These bricks are the sorrows, trials, and adversities that you encounter daily. Only as you look to Me will you have the strength to live a victoriously holy life on earth. I am your strength, your sustenance.

You cannot spiritually survive on earth without My Holy Spirit's leading. He guides you daily in right paths for My name's sake. As you heed and obey His voice, the path gets brighter before you and you learn to rejoice in God in all circumstances.

You are climbing the ladder to heaven. I am beneath you. I will catch you if you fall. I let you make the decision to raise to a higher level on the ladder by your obedient trust. I do not push or prod; I support and bless.

I am always here for you, but you must ask for My help to grow in grace. "Ask and you shall receive."

The way of the saints is arduous ad tricky. Satan seeks to trip you up around every corner. You must learn to discern his wiles. He remains hidden, not wanting to be discovered. You must unmask his intentions before all.

"Resist the devil and he will flee from you." Resist him in My name, in My strength, in My power.

I am equipping you to be a soldier of God, a holy knight of righteousness, upholding My kingdom of light for the world to see.

Stay faithful to where I've placed you. I am the essence of every situation and circumstance."

Jesus,
God's Revealer of Truth

July 10, 2018

"The sensibilities and responsibilities of a soul in love with Jesus are infinite. Horizons are broadened. Life takes on a new meaning, a new fragrance.

Life is not just a passing of time. It is a journey to your homeland, avoiding the pitfalls on the way. It is seeking to grow in intimacy with your Creator by daily walking in His company, as in the Garden of Eden.

God seeks fellowship and companionship. He seeks to reestablish what Adam and Eve destroyed.

God is love. He seeks true lovers, those that have cast all aside for love, as He did when He sent His only-begotten Son to die to reestablish His relationship with His children on earth.

God is faithful in His intentions. For centuries He has called out to men and women in every generation. He has walked with each soul ever born. Some have recognized Him; most have not, yet His faithfulness continues day by day.

God has called you to Himself. Your gratitude for this greatest of gifts should overwhelm you. So many souls have not heard what you hear, have not known what has been revealed to you.

You are highly favored by God when you sense the desire in your heart to love Him, to surrender yourself to Him in all things. This is His gift of love to you.

He has drawn you into the intimate circle of the Holy Trinity to allow you to fellowship with the uncreated God. There is no higher privilege.

Jesus Christ, true God and true man, is your friend, your advocate in the heavens. He speaks your name in love to the Father. He intercedes for you, asking God to make you strong in His grace and loving embrace.

You are greatly loved, children of God, those who know My name – Jesus, Savior of the world.

I am with you until the end of the age. Believe in My love for you. It is eternal joy in My Father's house.

The saints are praying for you. Thank them."

Jesus,
Eternal Joy of God to Man

July 12, 2018

"The power of a holy life is an unquenchable fire that rages in blazing flames to God most holy. Holiness and purity of heart draw God from heaven into your very small heart.

Righteousness, justice, kindness, compassion – traits of holiness won through prayer and intimacy with Jesus.

Spending time in the presence of God bears abundant fruits. Beautiful and virtuous thoughts arise, holy endeavors, grace-filled plans and activities proceed from a well-ordered and holy lifestyle.

He that is friends with the world cannot be My friend for the world loves sin. The world panders to the flesh, to sensuality and vice. "There is no fear of God before their eyes." They seek to please themselves, not their Creator, God Most Holy.

To be an intimate friend of God, you must spend much time in silent communion with Him. You must seek and find the silence in your life. You must open your mind and heart to another realm, the hidden spiritual realm, the world in which the saints and angels are watching and praying for you.

Loud souls do not hear God's voice. It is drowned out and muffled. There is no guidance to follow. The sensual self runs through life in confusion and distracting errors. A wise man seeks the silence, where he may meditate on the meaning of his existence. This silence humbles him and teaches him reverence for God.

The spiritually immature do not respect the grandeur of God because they have never met Him in the silence of their heart.

"Mary pondered all these things in her heart." Ask for the gift of silent pondering on God in your heart. Your heart will be stilled, and you will live in the presence of God's holy silence.

The silence will speak to you if you will allow it. It will tell you the story of a loving Father hovering lovingly over you, yearning for your love, obedience, and all-consuming attention to detail.

Ask Him to teach you His way of living. It is eternal peacefulness."

Jesus,
Master Teacher of Peace in God

"Purity of soul is extremely beautiful."

July 13, 2018

"I am calling you to a solitary road of prayer, of focus on the eternality of life. Just as cloistered orders live set apart from the world, I have called you to the solitary world of communion with Me amidst the distractions of life.

You must keep your eyes on the goal – eternal life in the City of Light. Nothing must matter to you anymore but your relationship with Me.

You must die to the world. You are walking a different highway – the highway to heaven. "You will walk with Me in white, for you are worthy."

Choose this path today. You will walk alone, but I will be with you. You will be filled with heavenly peace and joy. You will live on the heights, above the confusion of the world. You will go forward silently, without fanfare, alone but not lonely, growing daily in grace and holiness, ignored and mistreated by those who do not understand your path. My saints walked their paths alone, accompanied by the Holy Trinity.

Do you choose to walk this path with Me? It is the road of the blessed of My Father. You will be protected on all sides by Me, for many will try to thwart your journey. The darkness will turn into light before you.

You asked Me to broaden your horizons. I have opened to you the way to sainthood. It will take much renunciation and great purposeful effort, but your reward will be the intimacy with Me that you seek.

When you feel distracted or purposeless, close your eyes and see this holy road in your mind. It is the road of total abandonment to all I ask of you. It is a turning completely away from the world and its values. It is a new way of living, the life of the hermits and contemplatives that ran into the desert to be alone with Me.

Do you wish to live like this? If so, I will help you. The world needs saints of renunciation who live cloistered lives of prayer. They are saving the world by their immolation.

No more distractions. The road is before you. Start walking and do not stop until you reach the gates of the Eternal City of Light.

"It will be worth it all when you see Jesus."

Jesus,
Authority of God

July 14, 2018

"Each day man receives a choice of two directions: flesh or spirit. The spirit realm is invisible; therefore, it doesn't seem real to men. It must be searched for and sought out daily among manifold distracting forces that weigh it down, like wading through a muddy field to reach the desired destination. Few souls can tolerate the process. They give in to the pleasurable activities of this short earthly life to the detriment of their eternal souls.

The message of life is no longer heard in daily life. God's name is rarely spoken, except for blaspheming or cursing. Sacrificial souls are rare among the pleasure-seekers.

God's eyes roam to and fro throughout the earth seeking out the wise children who have sacrificed their earthly life in response to His great love, the love He showed by sending His beloved Son to earth to die for them. This beautiful sacrifice of the heart of God is no longer spoken of or cherished. Man's ingratitude is flagrant.

The heavens and all of creation shout out God's love in their beauty and order. The clouds reveal God's loving handiwork daily. The birds sing a song to God in the trees. All plants gravitate to the sun's energy, God's loving source of life.

Time spent loving and adoring your Creator is time spent gazing upon His loveliness as Source and Wellspring of all that exists.

As you acknowledge My presence, I bend down to your spirit to grant you the secrets of My heart. The angels bow in wonder at such a marvelous condescension – the grace of a God's love and mercy to fallen, iniquitous man.

Come live in My world, men of earth. You will find dazzling beauty, creative genius, peace beyond your understanding and the charm of a God beyond your deepest imaginings.

Those I have called to myself grow in My love daily. They are harassed by the Evil One, but they rush for refuge under My overshadowing wings of love. I protect them and give them a foretaste of life eternal.

What hope and joy My little ones experience daily! How they want to share My life with the world!

This short life will be over soon, My little and cherished saints. "Behold, I am coming soon."

Stay strong in your faith. Live in My love."

God,
Your Loving Father

July 16, 2018

"Contemplation in prayer draws you out of the realm of flesh into the realm of spirit. It is a magnet drawing your soul to your Source, God, your Creator.

Contemplation is a peaceful withdrawal from all that is earthly; matter becomes subject to spiritual laws. There is no other way to cross over into the higher realm than in silent contemplation of God.

"Be still and know that I am God." In this quiet of contemplation, you develop a 'knowing' beyond the intellect, beyond the capability to express in human language. Your spirit soars in the heavenlies, "seated in heavenly places with Christ Jesus."

Only My weaned and silent children come to know My heart. Many active souls do many wonderful works, but our relationship is employer to employee. I desire an intimate relationship with My children, where My heart becomes their heart, My desires become their desires. They serve Me joyously, compelled by My divine love operating within them.

These are My little children of divine love, the apple of My eye, abiding under the shadow of My omnipotent outstretched wings. I shelter them in My heart. They console Me for the ones that do not acknowledge My presence within them.

My love is a divine fire, a burning bush, engulfing all who approach its flames. "Our God is a consuming fire."

As you draw near to My heart of love, I allow its tenacity to grip your spirit. You then become a living flame of divine love.

Only by drawing near to the fire of love in My heart will you be permeated and, as it were, soaked in My heart of love. My goodness will become your goodness. My mercy and compassion will become your mercy and compassion.

I call all of you on earth to run into My open and welcoming arms of love. Allow Me to love you into My eternal kingdom. We will live in love throughout the never-ending ages of eternity.

What a prospect for your future! Find the silence to acquire this stupendous gift of eternal glory."

God,
Father of the Little Ones

July 17, 2018

"When I tear aside the veil from heaven to earth, the heart of man is inflamed with My love. This thick veil over mankind is self-absorption. Man cannot see past himself. He has a thick blanket of worries and cares compressing upon him on all sides. He cannot see heaven past his own problems.

When you come into My presence, you must cast aside all cares, worries, and thoughts of self. I will take your burdens upon My shoulders. Come to Me with a pure heart of love. Rivet your eyes upon Me alone. Forget yourself and think of Me and you will find Me.

I am God, yet I am also man. I think as a man and a God. I understand your thought processes, the difficulty of keeping your heart turned to the invisible world, your struggle against sin and being consumed by the world, your qualms and fears. Let everything go. Just come before Me and worship Me in spirit and in truth. I will reveal Myself to you; My great love for you, My wounded and rejected heart so sorely treated by those I have created.

I am calling you to sit in your seat "in heavenly places" so lovingly prepared for you. Only those who have died to self and the world can sit in these seats of glory in peace. They have left the world and its empty promises to pilgrim their way to My kingdom. They have borne the heat of the day. I have tested and tried them and have found them worthy to enter My heavenly court of love.

These are My true friends on earth, those who have made a commitment to Me and have proved themselves worthy of the prize of intimacy with the Godhead.

My special and privileged littlest ones know the greatest secrets of My heart. They speak to Me freely as friend to Friend. They know I love them, and they bask in this knowledge. They have left the world to follow Me, their highest and greatest Lord of all.

These littlest souls touch My heart. They are My predilection, My treasures on earth. Our fellowship is sweet, and My heart is comforted in them. They love Me and I love them. There is a mutual 'knowing' in our intimate encounters.

How easy it is to find God! Just love Him!"

Holy Spirit, Whisper of Holiness

July 20, 2018

"The souls of My littlest ones comfort My heart, so wounded by blasphemy and rejection. Mankind has walked away from Me and My commandments so lovingly given to preserve their lives. My commandments are not burdensome to those who love Me. They bring great peace and joy.

Man needs boundaries to thrive. Once the walls are thrown down, he feels helpless and vulnerable. He needs a shield of protection from harm, from enemies within and without, from himself and his excesses.

I placed man on earth in a garden in paradise. I gave him all he needed for a joyful and contented existence in fellowship with Me. He broke My loving commandment, choosing to tear down the walls of our friendship. I came to earth to repair the breach, to open the communication with God again, to set souls free from the bondage they had enclosed themselves in.

In love, I descended to earth in the highest act of humility. I chose a stable with animals for My birthplace. I was unknown and rejected. Finally, they put Me to death. I took all your punishment for sin upon Myself to gather you all together as a shepherd his wayward and erring flock. The door to heaven was opened. All who chose to enter were welcomed with heavenly joy.

As the centuries rolled on, My message became fainter and fainter to men. Heroic souls soon became hard to find. Role models became scarce.

In this day, sin is the norm. Few and far between are found pure and holy souls, those little ones that have kept themselves unspotted from the world.

These littlest ones gather around My altar bearing gifts of humility and obedience. They have shunned the world's sinfulness. They set themselves apart exclusively to love, serve, follow, and honor Me alone. I shed My light on earth through their holy countenances and serene movements through time. They perfume the air when they enter a dwelling.

They are unknown on earth, but well known in heaven. Their prayers fly like arrows to the throne of grace. Their wishes are God's priority, for the Holy Spirit inspires their prayers.

O My beloved Littlest Ones, stay strong. Stay away from the world's sirens, calling you to dissipation and worldliness. You are not of the world. Separate yourself and live in My holiness. You are My treasures on earth, My jewels gleaming in My eye.

How I love you, for you have loved Me in abandon."

Jesus,
Lover

July 23, 2018

"Holiness demands respect and reverence. The sacredness of God's dwelling place on earth has been profaned and rejected. How few frequent the holy places on earth, the sacred ground where the divine Savior of the world resides in the Tabernacle of Love on earth.

I have promised to be with you always and I have kept My promise. I come to you as mere bread and wine which has been transformed into My divine Body and Blood on earth.

The priests of the old covenant reverently handled the sacred articles. How is My flesh handled in these days of sacrilegious offenses?

If men only understood what is before them, veiled by earthly matter, revered in the heavens. Like snowflakes that vanish at the touch of a warm hand, My intangible presence vanishes at the touch of fleshly ignorance. I am to be delicately handled by My people or I will disappear before their eyes when I experience profanations.

Those who truly love Me know how to approach My sensitive heart. They humbly and lovingly come before Me with love in their eyes, not expecting from Me, but coming to give Me something – themselves.

They gaze upon My loveliness in silence. My glory rushes in upon them. They truly come to know as they are known.

My littlest ones are My charming darlings on earth, My sheep of predilection. They follow Me obediently, not straying from the path of holiness but staying true to the course. I turn to look at them, ragged and shaggy from life's troubles, but with eager and ardent eyes of love they keep their eyes fixed on Me. I hear their steps behind Me, faltering and shaky, yet persistent to keep pace with Me.

We are the holy band of travelers to My Father's kingdom. My cross bearers follow Me up the hill to Calvary. They lay down their burdens at the foot of My holy cross. There I open the door to My Father's kingdom. There they shall rejoice forevermore.

My friends on earth rejoice My heart. They shall walk with Me in white for they are worthy.

"My sheep hear My voice. I know them, and they follow Me."

Jesus,
Heavenly Sheep Herder

July 25, 2018

"What is the cross? It is the adversity governed and allowed by God to form you into a holy saint of God.

A cross can be despised, endured, neglected, or thrown away in despair. A cross can be mistrusted, misapplied, and turned into a tragedy instead of a blessing.

Crosses are the jewels you will offer to God in His heavenly dwelling. Being conformed into the image of His Son, Jesus, is being transformed into His image resting upon a cross between heaven and earth, the bridge of love God has suspended from heaven.

A cross can and will become a great blessing to you if you share it with Jesus, the yoke bearer. He is your Teacher to guide you into all truth, but many life changes can only be changed by the power of the holy cross.

To be despised on earth, like the Son of God, is the greatest honor in the life of a Christian. To be poor, lowly, misunderstood, persecuted, humbled, and broken is to carry the beloved cross of Jesus, as He ascends the hill to Calvary to atone for the sins of the world.

Cross bearers are the best friends of Jesus, His intimate circle of holy friends, who stand by Him in the day of trouble. They do not scatter when troubles arise. They stand close to their Brother, Jesus, in His trials and adversities borne for the sins of the world.

They have heavenly vision and despise the things of earth. They remain on the cross with Jesus, bearing His shame and reproach, bringing many sons to glory with Him.

Jesus has few friends willing to bear the cross <u>with</u> Him for the souls of men. Men want to be admired, respected, flattered, and praised. To be despised on earth is their greatest fear.

If only they had heavenly vision! They would run fervently and eagerly to the crosses Jesus sends them, to bear them lovingly and patiently beside Him, their love and friendship consoling His wounded and abandoned heart.

Love the cross, men of earth. It is truly God's gift to His beloved and chosen best friends on earth!

There will be no crosses in heaven. Now is your only time to show Jesus that you love Him more than yourself by throwing all on earth to the wayside and joyfully picking up the cross of Jesus as a true friend would."

Holy Spirit,
Lover of Jesus

August 1, 2018

"The saints look upon the face of the all-holy God in light inaccessible. As they gaze, they are continually transformed into His light. To gaze upon God is to become light, an indefinable heavenly essence.

Your realm is touched with God's light. God's realm is light. His light pierces the veil between heaven and earth.

God's light burns away the dross of your sins. It cleanses, purifies, enkindles, and transforms all it touches. Sin blocks the light of God and His transforming power and touch.

God's saints are vessels of light bringing God into the atmosphere of darkness on earth. Their presence diffuses God's light, bringing a holy fragrance and a divine warmth to all situations.

The devil runs from the light of God. He hates the light. He roams in darkness, creating havoc and disunion wherever he goes. The light bearers are his nemesis. He mocks and scorns their purity, for light is diffused through purity and cleanness of heart.

Run from sin, My children. Do not block the holy light of God.

Light makes the plants on earth grow. Without light, they wither and die. So it is with the souls of men. Without God's light, they wither and die.

Step out into the sunshine of My love. Let My light permeate every cell of your body into the fibers of your eternal soul.

"Let your light so shine before men that they may see your good works and glorify your Father in heaven."

Light produces righteousness and a holy life. Walk in this purity and your light will shine brightly before men. They will be drawn to the light of God. This will save their souls from death.

What a great responsibility for My souls, to walk in My light!

You will reap an abundant harvest of souls if you live your life in God's light daily."

Holy Spirit, Light Bearer

August 2, 2018

"Turning your back on the world to follow Me is a holy calling to set out on the highway of holiness, the road of God, set apart for the saints to heroically tread in the midst of a nonbelieving world.

Noah turned his back on the world. He was ridiculed and taunted. My disciples turned their backs on the world. They were martyred. Saints in every century suffered much tribulation when they set out to follow in the footsteps of the suffering Christ. Their love for Me took away all desire for the world and its ways. I became their life choice. I became their ambition. Everything on earth lost its charm. To live in the earth's atmosphere became burdensome because they tasted heavenly wonders and delights.

To turn your back on the world is to live every moment of your life gazing into My eyes of love. It is forgetting yourself completely because you become lost in My love. It is to live a heavenly life on earth. It means giving Me your time on earth, not pursuing fleshly pursuits. It means trusting in My daily plan for you, obediently following My directives, humbling yourself beneath every occurrence in your daily life.

I long for this intimate relationship with you. So few souls truly find Me. They know about Me, yet they do not personally know Me as friend and lover.

I can be as close and as real to you as you allow Me to be. Including Me in your life is your decision.

I do everything possible to reveal My heart to you daily, but you have a free will to accept or reject My advances.

A simple "I love You" in the purity of your heart draws Me to you immediately. I am not a God far away. I am within you, waiting to be acknowledged.

O, the humility of a God begging for your friendship! My love compels Me to seek longingly for the love of My children whom I have created with such loving care.

I love every soul I have created, even the most sinful and the most evil who reject Me vehemently. I long for their return to My merciful heart.

Be with Me. Do not leave Me alone. I need friends to appreciate My overtures. Rejection is wounding, and I have been rejected in the houses of My friends through the centuries.

Will you be a friend of the God who loves you infinitely? You do not see Me, yet you love Me with My gift of love to you. Explore this gift, for it will bring you to glory in a flash, like lightning.

Explore My love."

Jesus,
Lover of Souls

August 3, 2018

"Streams and rays of heavenly graces and blessings are enveloping My people as they kneel reverently before Me. I look upon each child of faith before Me with such joy in My heart. Never having seen My face, they love Me fervently.

This is the mystery in God's heart from the foundation of the world, a mystery formed in the heart of God who can do all things. What greater love story could have transpired? A God humbling Himself to love and save His wandering and oppressed children.

My heart is all love. I am so misunderstood by mankind. Man's heart was made in God's image. He has a choice to accept or reject My love. That is the gift of free will given to man by My Father.

I have called the littlest ones to Myself. The humble and lowly charm My heart, for they follow in My footsteps of pure love. I desire to be loved by My children ... loved for who I am, loved as a friend and loved as a Savior. Those who truly love Me find the greatest treasure found on earth. They enter heaven's time, and eternity is theirs. They will live in endless bliss with Me and My Father.

Children, love Me as I love My Father. My Father's will was My food on earth. Every moment of My life on earth was spent adoring My Father and seeking His good pleasure. If I am your Father, if I have given My life for you, should I expect less of you, O distracted souls on earth?

Canonized saints had one quality above everything – love for God alone. God was absolutely everything to them. There were no halfway measures with them. "All for God" was their heart cry.

Love alone draws you quickly into the heart of My Father. Love Him and He will do the rest. Trust in His love and watchcare over your life.

"Love is not loved" was the lament of many saints. Their hearts were grieved at the lack of love for God among souls, even those of His children that claimed to love Him.

Love is shown in action – holiness of life, disciplined alone time with God, living in love.

These are My children of grace, standing alone in a world given over to sensuality and evil. How I love them! My faithful children!

It is in these silent hours of enjoying My presence when the most work is done in your soul. I impress My image upon your spirit. We become one.

Adore and see the grandeur of your God of sacrifice."

Jesus,
Sacrificed for Love of You

August 7, 2018

"Your heart is overwhelmed by your sins and you have brought this burden to the only One that can really help you. Man does not have answers. He strives to be the master and the teacher, but he is only a child coursing his way through life, having no control whatsoever.

I am the Light of the world. I make the path plain before you. I am your sure refuge in distress. Do not put your hope or confidence in man, for he is very weak and frail. He is a tottering reed that flails in the wind of tribulation and anxiety.

Come to Me with your heavy burdens of shame and guilt and I will lift them from your shoulders. The load is too heavy for you to carry. I will be your partner in life. I will bear the yoke beside you, holding up the heavier end.

When you put your trust in people, be sure that they will disappoint you. They cannot live up to the expectations of a God who knows your destiny.

Trials should send you quickly to My heart. There is your port and refuge in every storm. I am a kind Creator. I know you are frail, that you are made of dust and ashes, that your will is weak and changeable. I want you to rely on My guidance, on My strength, on My perfect designs for your life.

I will never disappoint you. If you come to Me, I will help you and set you again on the right path. I care for your soul more than you do.

Lack of trust wounds My heart, and so many of My friends do not run to Me for support. They turn to the world which has no answers.

You can talk to many people about your troubles and you will hear a different point of view from each one. Not so with your Creator – you can be sure that He is Truth, and He will show you the way to live your life abundantly in His presence.

"He came unto His own and His own received Him not." What a sad state of affairs!

I am here for you. Come to Me, My children."

Jesus,
Comforter

August 8, 2018

"Breathe in My Essence. Breath and air are My mysterious elements to keep your soul living. My air keeps you alive moment by moment. If you were hurled into the atmosphere of outer space, you would die. My air is a gift to planet earth.

What is air? I called My Holy Spirit the breath of God. My Holy Spirit of air keeps your planet in existence. As you breathe in air to live, so can you breathe in the Holy Spirit. As you open yourself without obstacle or hindrance, you open the passageway for Him to enter your spirit in His fullness. It is as simple as breathing.

Sit alone in My presence and allow the Holy Spirit to breathe through you. Allow Him full access to all that you are. Release your hold on everything. Let Him take full control. He will breathe the breath of Jesus into your soul to animate you with holy and heavenly desires. He will capture your heart and your will, making of you a devoted disciple. He will fill you with the peace and contentment of Jesus. He will become your life-breath.

You will walk the earth breathing the air of heaven, the pure air of obedience and dedication to the Father's will in all things. You will soar above the earth on the wings of the wind, God's holy breath of love.

Breathe in My presence moment by moment. Say in your heart: "I am breathing in my God. I desire to live on His breath alone.""

"Draw near to God and He will draw near to you."
There is no closer union than breathing another's breath
in. You will be quickened by the motions of the Holy Spirit
dwelling within you.

I blew My breath into Adam's nostrils and he became
a living soul. Allow Me to breathe My breath into your
soul. You will become a living epistle of My holiness."

Jesus,
God's Breath,
The Word Made Flesh

August 15, 2018

"My sweetest Mother loves you as her own child. I have given her a unique role in salvation history. She is the human mother of the human race. I have exalted her to this position because of My great love and respect for her as My Mother on earth.

You could not find a better mother to emulate, a better role model to pattern yourself after. She desires to teach you her ways – to bring you with her into the very heart of God, to His Trinitarian intimacy. She is a real and sure guide for you to follow.

She is bringing many sons and daughters to glory by her intercessory prayers for them. She goes to her Son daily to intercede for the saints on earth. God has given her a unique intercessory role in the heavens.

Her purity, her luminous faith, her grace-filled actions all won God's heart. She is His masterpiece, an obedient daughter of faith.

She will guide you to God quickly if you will allow it. God's throne of grace is always open for her to plead the cause of a soul lost on earth.

Intimacy with Mary is intimacy with her Son. The bond between them is so strong that when you solicit Mary's prayers, you are also calling Jesus to your aid.

There is no fear of taking away from the glory of Jesus. She is everything to Jesus. When you honor His Mother, He is honored.

Talk things over with My Mother. Give yourself to her. She will guide you to holiness quickly and surely.

She is the most blessed forever Virgin of Virgins in the heavens. Embrace her heavenly role as Mediatrix of all Graces."

Holy Spirit,
Spouse of Mary,
God's Masterpiece

August 16, 2018

"Religion is a spectacle of God's grace among men. Man needs an anchor in his soul, for he is bobbing about on the agitated waters of the darkened sea of humanity. He needs guidance to know how to follow God, how to please God, how to act in this world as God would have him live.

People have thrown off the yoke of their father's oppressive religion, as they call it. What has ensued is utter chaos and destruction in lives, in families, in marriages, and in society in general. Each has followed his own path. There is no unity of spirit or cooperation among the people of the land. There is hatred, greed, animosity, and slander. The news agencies spout out the negative consequences of sinful lifestyles on the hour.

The children seek guidance from their electronic devices, none of which are monitored. The parents are absorbed in luxurious lifestyles, abdicating their leadership roles which have been taken over by the media. Politicians lie and promise falsehoods. Television is a cesspool of sin and degradation. The airwaves blast forth blasphemies against God and man. This sinful generation is on its way to a ruin that is beyond repair.

God's grace lingers hopefully over despairing hearts, but the thick darkness of sins hides His rays of love. "How narrow is the way to life, and few there be that find it." Those few are holding up the pillars of the earth by their holy prayers and tears.

I have called forth an army of mourners on earth, mourning and wailing for the sins of the world, as mourners mourn at a funeral. They have the weeping heart of Jesus, weeping over the hardheartedness of men towards His ever-sacrificing love for them.

The wounded fall by the wayside with no one to lift them up. There are no souls to give answers to the depressed masses. My elect are not filled with the Holy Spirit. His power is inactive within them because of their lukewarm lifestyles.

So few of My chosen ones are available for Me to speak to the masses of hungry sheep in the world, to speak forth My Word with power, to heal the sick, to bless souls with My holy gifts.

Only those that know the Master can shepherd souls in truth. They allow Me to work through them. They get out of the way by dying to themselves.

I will shepherd My sheep through My lowly souls filled with great love for Me. They are My mouthpiece to this world of woe. They love Me, and I use them to show forth My glory. They are My holy vessels of honor "fit for the Master's use", bringing many souls to glory along with them. They have lost their lives in this world to keep them unto life eternal. How I love them!"

Jesus,
Lover of the Littlest Ones

August 17, 2018

"Draw near to God and He will draw near to you." Your God is an excellent Father, desiring to protect, lead, guide, and shelter His beloved children. He hears their cries for help and responds immediately. "Ask and you shall receive," He graciously speaks to His little ones.

God desires friends, obedient lovers that respond immediately to His graces. He loves a cheerful countenance, a kind disposition, a humble life, a simple directness in actions. God does not like pride, arrogance, or duplicity. "Arrogance is odious to the Lord." He gives His graces only to the humble of heart. Those that test His goodness wound His tender heart.

"God seeks worshippers that worship Him in spirit and truth." He reveals Himself to the pure in heart. He leans down from heaven to favor His chosen ones, those that have given up their lives in this world for Him.

God is gentle and kind, amiable and sweet, compassionate, merciful, and forgiving. All that come to Him in meekness are received. God is meek, and He loves to live among meek souls.

God is a wonderful artist, creative, and sometimes amusing in His creations. He loves variety and color, different forms, textures, and shapes. He loves to create something beautiful out of nothing.

He loves to reshape and beautify useless or broken-down images.

He loves to fashion saints out of the greatest sinners. His mercy shines forth spectacularly when He changes a hardened sinner into a model of virtue, His icon of grace.

God is love. If you love, you will find Him quickly. God is drawn to love. If love is your watchword, you will be filled with God.

God is Spirit. To reach Him, you must speak from your spirit. His Spirit will touch your spirit and you will be gloriously transformed into His likeness on earth. These spirit guides transform the world. They bring God to earth for men to behold.

"Deep calleth unto deep ..." The Spirit within you is crying out for union with God. Surrender all to His embrace.

Give all to receive all. It is in the simplicity of complete abandonment and surrender that you will find God living the life of Christ within you."

Holy Spirit,
God's Love to Men

August 20, 2018

"The birds of the air do not worry about their food supply. They live in total trust. I desire that My children trust Me with the same abandon. I have promised to lead and guide you if you place yourself in My hands. Trust that I have heard your petitions and that I will answer your prayers.

Go forward in peace trusting My guidance. Do not lose your peace or look for answers from your own experience.

I alone know the answer to your every concern. Entrust all your cares to Me and I will speedily set to work on them.

Less talking and more trust. Live in peace of soul, leaving all the details to Me. Total trust brings peace of soul and a knowing assurance that all will be well. Much talking and reasoning is futile. I alone have all the answers in life. I see the big picture, the eternal landscape.

Life is a rugged journey for souls. You encounter precipices continuously as you climb the mountain of holiness. In peace of soul, keep your eyes on the top of the mountain, your ascent to the heights, knowing that I walk beside you, making your path safe. Trust that I am your journeying partner, pointing out the correct turns at the crossroads.

My hand will lead and guide you all the days of your life's journey. Clasp My hand trustingly. Do not worry or fret; instead turn to Me in prayer, bringing Me all the petitions in your heart

I am faithful in all My dealings with you. You can count on My help.

I am the ever-faithful Jesus, the Savior of mankind. I offer you abundant living if you walk daily with Me.

Take My hand. We will journey together to your eternal homeland."

Jesus,
Traveler on the Road of Life

August 21, 2018

"To love with My love is your highest calling. Many souls love others with a human love, a natural love, that emotionally offers assistance and support. This is good in itself, but to love with My love is the touchstone of the spiritual heights.

To walk with Jesus is to be embraced in His love. This love infiltrates and permeates every cell in your body, bringing light and life to your genetic structure. This love is a fountain of life, a wellspring of God's goodness, springing up from within your spirit.

God loves all that He has created, yet the souls that accept His love in all its fullness walk the path of Jesus on earth. His light explodes from within them. All they touch is sanctified and consecrated to be used for holy purposes.

They are living icons of Jesus in the world, walking in holiness, speaking words of truth, healing and restructuring broken humanity.

How rare are the souls that truly allow God to fully possess them! Men hold back themselves from receiving God's grace of Himself. He cannot fill a sinful, sensual, carnal soul in love with the sinful world. These souls wander in darkness, filled with the world's frivolities, lukewarm, carnal, and desolate. They do not live the abundant life that has been promised to them. They neglect their soul and pamper their body. They refuse the instruction of the Holy Spirit, urging them to repent and choose God as their life's companion.

How I long to fill My children with My goodness! How I delight in My pure children of love, those that gaze upon Me daily with a simple will to love, serve, and follow Me! They are the apple of My eye. They shall rule and reign with Me eternally. They possess My heart and all that I am!

What an honor to be the friend of God, His noble child of excellence, a saint on earth!

The angels marvel at My condescension – to make saints out of sinful men on earth.

I show forth My glory in My mercy to the men of earth. The angels are astounded and delighted.

Those that seek My face <u>shall</u> find Me. I am staring into your eyes as we speak."

God of Glory

August 22, 2018

"Jesus must be everything to you in this life. Your being exists in Him. All who possess the Son possess life, for He is the source of all that exists.

Jesus is the incarnate Deity visiting His creation in love. He resides in humility in the tabernacle before the altar of His holy sacrifice. His love is endless. All who come to this fount of mercy are satiated with His fullness.

You are seated in the throne room of God, unaware of what is going on spiritually around you. Hosts of glorious angels bow reverently before Jesus, the King of life on earth. Mortal souls are blindly oblivious to the glory of this house of God.

Two worlds are going on here. The mortal path of trust and abandonment meets the veiled world of another realm, the spirit world. Only he who has eyes to see by faith will understand the dignity of this holy temple.

Faith is the key that opens the door to the reality of what is really happening on earth. As your faith increases, your eyes become clearer to see what really matters in your life.

Homage to Jesus is your life purpose, returning sacrificial love in response to sacrificial love.

You have been brought here "for such a time as this." Though your path seems futile at times, know that all has a purpose in My plans for you.

Stay the course. Be faithful in the little things, for some day I will entrust you with far bigger things.

This is kingdom work, accomplished in secret upon earth, but known well in the eternal realm of light.

Look to Me that you might be radiant with My light. I will give you My vision, My eternal perspective, My kingdom plan. So few entrust themselves to kingdom work in this world of sensual pleasures!

In the quietness you will hear My voice which will make you wise unto salvation. How lovely to be listened to by attentive souls! My heart is full of the wisdom of the ages. How I long to share Myself with My children on earth!

I am Jesus, your life. Come to Me to find the abundant life you are seeking so mindlessly. My paths are truth."

Jesus,
Your Older and Wiser Brother of Earth

August 24, 2018

"Life is a series of struggles upon struggles. It is a growth period, a time to mature spiritually. I know the needs of your spirit. Growth pains are challenging and somber, but if accepted and understood, they yield great fruit.

There is such a lack of trust in My teaching methods. Each lesson is unique to the individual. I know what is needed to teach eternal truths. I know what is needed to sanctify a soul. Nothing escapes My notice. Nothing happens by chance. Do you believe this?

I desire that you see every occurrence from an eternal perspective. Life is short, and eternity is forever. I cut away the cancerous lesions of sin from those who seek to follow in My footsteps. It is painful and prolonged at times, but in the end, the lesson is learned, and you see why things occurred as they did.

The lesson is trust. Rejoice in My will for you in trust that I do all things well. If I leave you as you are, you will never grow in holiness. Sometimes drastic measures are needed to stop a soul in its tracks. Some lessons are faint, prolonged, and tedious, teaching the lesson of patient endurance.

Trust and abandonment to all that happens will keep you in serenity and you will possess great peace of soul. Entrust your children and grandchildren to My care. I love them more than you do. I will always do what is best for them physically as well as spiritually.

Rejoicing in trials and tribulations is a hallmark of great saints. It takes many years to get to this high degree of sanctity, but if you persevere in fidelity daily, you will see the fruits of these painful experiences. You will understand the delays, the fits and starts, the confusion and the obscurity surrounding every problem.

I work intricately in the most mundane circumstances. I am forming saints on earth and this involves struggle upon struggle to bring it to completion.

Save yourself the trouble of an anguished heart by trusting that My perfect will is being accomplished in your life and in the lives of your loved ones.

You know you can trust My judgments. Your life experiences have proved My faithfulness to you."

Jesus,
Faithful Friend

August 27, 2018

"In the silence you will find God. Words tell you about God, but silence reveals Him as He is. The senses are a barrier and a blockade that impede you from entering the Holy of Holies. "God is spirit, and those who worship Him must worship Him in spirit and in truth."

To die to yourself is to stop using words and deeds to find God. It is to die to the fleshly way of seeking God. Your body is an encumbrance of sorts when it comes to entering the spiritual realm of God. He is beyond all conceptions you have of Him. He is gloriously transcendent, above all you could ever grasp in your human faculties.

To die to yourself means to turn your back on the world, to seek solitude and silence, to hush your words and thoughts, to love the stillness, to seek the solitary moments of God's presence, to restrain your natural pursuit of restless activity, to quiet your curiosity, to quell your thoughts – basically to be alone with God in the stillness, beyond thoughts and words.

This is contemplation, an art completely unknown to modern man in his restless pursuits. Man is always trying to prove himself to himself and others. That is pride in action. You are a dust creature, sustained by God's breath every moment of your existence. Seek Him and you shall truly live!

The world has nothing to offer you but anxiety and trouble. Pleasures do not last. They are fleeting.

Happiness is a vague future hope. Only holiness of life will give you the inner joy you desire.

I am the source of abundant living. Come to Me to be satiated with eternal riches and eternal joys. All that come to Me I will in no wise send away.

I am longing for you to become wise, My children. Seek the pearl of great price. Sell all you have to obtain it and then live your life holding it high before you as a lantern of hope, following the light to the Eternal City above, where I await your eternal felicity and bliss.

I am faithful and true. I am the pearl of great price."

Jesus,
Treasure of God to Mankind

August 28, 2018

"Though you fall over and over again, I desire that you continually come running into My arms with a repentant heart.

Your falls surprise you and dishearten you, I know, but that is the human condition. The mark of a saint is the continual rising up from misery and failure to repentant forgiveness and deep trust in My mercy.

So many souls do not like their state in life. They want the life of another soul. Yet they do not understand that I have chosen their unique state in life to sanctify them personally. And there will always without doubt be a soul carrying a heavier cross!

You must trust that all happens for a reason in My divine plan. You must acquiesce moment by moment to what I bring into your life, a smiling 'yes' at every fork in the road.

True saints do not wonder why things happen. They say, "It is the Lord" in all things. They have died to themselves, so these occurrences become indifferent to them.

Souls still holding tightly to self become alarmed at change. They see things from an earthly viewpoint. They do not realize that God uses human instruments to teach His children holy living.

Go forward valiantly in spite of your falls. It will all come out right in the end when God reveals to you His intricate designs on your behalf.

The tapestry of your life will be turned over and all the knotted and dangling loose threads you have encountered will be the most beautiful colors in the finished tapestry masterpiece. You will then understand what is now obscure.

Please trust Me. I have your best interests at heart."

Jesus,
Your Best Friend

August 29, 2018

"Life is a series of decisions regarding your actions. You are to live an upright and godly life, staying grounded on a holy path. Many obstacles will distract you from this goal, but you must press on, forward to the eternal goal.

All souls do not have this goal. They are on a different path. They are not interested in holy living or to be set apart for My use in the world.

You must not let these souls sidetrack you from your relationship with Me by destroying your peace or allowing them to pull you into their problems, the ones they have chosen as a life plan. They need to suffer the consequences of their actions to learn what I must teach them on their journey.

So many well-meaning children of Mine neglect their own sanctity while trying to save others from their perplexities. Each individual is responsible for each decision made, whether right or wrong.

There are consequences to each decision. You cannot take the consequences or responsibilities from another soul without greatly harming their maturity, spiritual or physical maturity.

Some day every soul will have to answer for all the life choices they have made. You cannot step in to quell the pain. It is harmful to not allow souls to learn the painful lesson of living with the consequences of their actions.

Your goodwill is not necessarily My will. You must let Me lead you in all your endeavors to mitigate another's pain. I might tell you to look to yourself and your own interests as I did to Peter on that day when he inquired about John's destiny.

Do not be discouraged. I know you mean well in trying to help but meaning well and doing the right thing doesn't always coincide. Sometimes doing the right thing is painful and it hurts, but discipline heals a wayward lifestyle. You must allow Me to discipline My children without interfering with your good intentions.

You do well to come to Me for instructions. You recognize your weaknesses and know that you need My strength. I willingly help you and will lead you forth in righteousness to solve all these daily problems.

Let Me decide for you who to help and who not to help. Ask Me and I will surely let you know.

This will bring you great peace."

Jesus,
Universal Father

August 30, 2018

"Daily resolutions to do better please Me greatly. So many souls do not know the state of their spirituality. So many do not care to find out.

To know Me is to want to please Me in all things, to improve, to grow in grace and holiness daily. That is the reason for your existence – to grow into the likeness of Jesus Christ, the all-holy Savior.

Life is a daily struggle against the world, the flesh, and the devil. These are formidable opponents and catch you unawares. Only with My strength and foresight can you conquer your weak and unstable condition, which is the lot of every human.

If you stay in My presence, you will be aware of your surroundings and the pitfalls waiting to entrap you. You will know how to resist the devil and his subtle strategies.

Your only answer to conquer in life is to abide in Me moment by moment, to turn to Me incessantly for guidance and direction, to trust My judgments as to what is occurring in your life daily.

Prayer warriors are valiant, for they live in Me. They keep the connection to the spiritual realm alive and real. I infuse Myself into them and they thrive with My life and My strength.

Keep coming to Me when you fall, when you sin, when you are burdened, when you need help and directions, when you need a lift. I am always here for you with all the wisdom you need.

I am your self-esteem, your stability, your guide through life, the answer to every one of your problems. Trust in My great love for you and never stop running to Me in your perplexities and confusing labors.

I am the Great Psychologist of the ages. I know all the answers."

Jesus,
Psychology Major

"Love is the summit of the mountain you are climbing to sanctity."